Simply Hell let Loose

stories of Australians at War

Published by ABC Books for the
AUSTRALIAN BROADCASTING CORPORATION
GPO Box 9994 Sydney NSW 2001

Copyright © Department of Veterans' Affairs 2002

First published September 2002

The National Library of Australia
Cataloguing-in-Publication entry
  Simply hell let loose : stories of Australians at war.
  ISBN 0 7333 1078 8.
  1. Australia - History, Military. I. Australian
  Broadcasting Corporation. II. Australia. Dept. of
  Veterans' Affairs.
994

Designed by vossdesign
Seperations by *Shannon Books, Melbourne*
Printed and bound in Australia by *Shannon Books, Melbourne*

Cover images
Corporal L Hollier of Hunters Hill, NSW, writing a letter, north of Alexishafen,
New Guinea, 5 June 1944. AWM 017230.
Gunner Ronald Sinclair.

Simply Hell let Loose

stories of Australians at War

Department of Veterans' Affairs

Dug-Outs at Anzac Cove Dardanelles

FOREWORD

For more than a century, Australian men and women have willingly answered the call to defend our shores and the freedom and democracy we value so highly. From South Africa to East Timor, Gallipoli to Afghanistan, and on the home front, Australians have a proud and distinguished record of service in times of war and conflict.

Since Federation, Australia has placed great importance on recording our wartime history, from facts and figures through to historical and social analysis of wars, campaigns and battles. However, our records should also include the personal stories of the men and women who experienced first-hand the horrors, victories, defeats and mateship of war.

Within these pages you will find the range and depth of human emotion – from fear to exhilaration, sadness and loss to joy, as well as the occasional chuckle. The stories told here are not simply those of the bravest or best. They are, however, typical of the experiences of many Australians.

They are drawn from the many contributions collected during the development of the acclaimed 'Australians at War' television series. Just as it helped to fund that series, the Federal Government is equally proud to support *Simply Hell Let Loose* and provide an opportunity for more Australians to learn of the experiences of our servicemen and women in defence of our nation and our values.

In telling their stories, veterans and their families are helping to preserve these experiences for future generations. They are a part of our national heritage. I encourage all Australians to preserve their own family's wartime memorabilia and history – these help us understand what it means to be Australian.

Each story is unique, a precious fragment of the collective experience of Australians at war. It is my hope that you will enjoy this collection and find it as compelling and memorable to read as I did.

Danna Vale

The Hon Danna Vale MP
Minister for Veterans' Affairs

SIMPLY HELL LET LOOSE

War is intensely personal. Battles may be fought between large armies, fleets of ships or squadrons of aircraft, but the lives of individuals, at the front, in support and at home are affected. At the time, many of these servicemen and women and their loved ones record their impressions in diaries or letters, or years later set down their recollections to share with family and friends. Reading two or more accounts of the same event, the differences in detail in each report are often striking. Anecdotes help bring to life a story in a way that official records and facts do not. The personal story, the eyewitness account, never fails to enthral: 'I was there and this is what I saw and felt.'

In 2001, the television documentary series 'Australians at War' was broadcast on ABC Television to mark Australia's Centenary of Federation. Funded by the Federal Government, the series recounted the experiences of Australians in times of war and conflict, from the Boer War to today's United Nations peacekeeping operations, and examined how these have helped to shape Australia's development as a nation.

The series producers, commissioned by the Department of Veterans' Affairs (DVA), began with a wealth of information at their disposal: histories, both official and unauthorised; countless books written by unit associations, academics and individuals from the most famous wartime leaders down to unknown servicemen and women; newspapers, photographs and newsreels. But it was personal stories that were identified as the key to producing a successful series.

DVA, in collaboration with ABC Radio, launched the Great Search, inviting Australian veterans and their families to come forward with their own wartime memorabilia to be used in the series. More than 1,800 responses were received in a treasure trove of letters, diaries, photographs and other pieces. With every piece came somebody's story, the recollections of an Australian who survived the experience of war, or the treasured memories of a family whose loved one didn't come home.

Simply Hell Let Loose now draws on that storehouse of stories. Not all items received by DVA could be included. More are available online at www.australiansatwar.gov.au. The selection encompasses all of the major conflicts in which Australia took part in the twentieth century.

Set among stories of the brave and gallant are stories of ordinary people doing their bit in extraordinary times, and everyday, almost routine, accounts of life in places where they struggled to survive.

From the naked Anzacs at Gallipoli to the Aussie peacekeeper in the Sinai; from the brutalised prisoners of war of Changi to the British Commonwealth Occupation Force troops serving in occupied Japan; from the Land Army girl to the mother still writing letters to a son whose fate she may never know; these stories give readers a glimpse of the contributions made by those on the front line and at home, who have served our nation in wartime.

CONTENTS

Boer War

Cecil kept his hat on   1

'Simply Hell let Loose'   7

'The first Australian to fall in action in S.A.'   13

World War I

'Come on Australians, show these French and British beggars how to fight'   17

'I'm a very lucky pusson, for shore!'   21

'An abominable itch'   27

Protecting the name of Anzac   31

The war in the desert on horseback   37

'Weather beautiful. Health indifferent. Prospects bright. Spirits High'   45

'Please accept my sincerest sympathy & admiration for your brave young boy'   51

'We'll all be together again before the next Xmas'   55

'Like putting up cardboard nine-pins in a hurricane'   59

Aboriginal boy survives family massacre but dies in war   67

World War II

'The Kelly Gang' rides again   71

'Jeese, I thought you was the cook!'   75

'It really was a terrible day'   79

'I hope I never have to live through another day like today'   83

'Our Government had sold them the scrap iron, but they brought it back!'   89

'May you soon come back to us all'   93

'The most wonderful news we have ever had'   99

Tough entry requirements for the Late Arrivals Club   103

47 days in a leaky boat   113

'One thing more—goodbye'   121
Hugging the ground in New Guinea   127
The accidental coastwatcher   133
No waltzing after Matilda hit mine   139
'Devotion to duty worthy of the highest praise'   141
'The army ahead of the army'   147
Rewarding and worthwhile life in the Women's Land Army   151
Knitters! Please Take Notice   155
'1236 Diver cut Saigon–Singapore cable'   159
'Our hell on earth'   163
'Hiroshima is rapidly returning to life'   171

The Korean War
Flying Mustangs over Korea   179
'What a beautiful target'   189
Preparing for a nice easy shoot   197

Vietnam and South-East Asia
War correspondents without a war   201
Minesweeper patrols during Indonesian Confrontation   205
'We worked and lived in a killing zone'   209
'You must be paid a fortune to work here'   213
'Vietnam's Rolls Royce dealer, 106 Field Workshop'   221

The Gulf War and Peacekeeping
'The most intensive and exciting period'   225
'Making a contribution to world politics'   233

CECIL KEPT HIS HAT ON

Trooper Cecil E Ewens
South Australian Bushmen's Contingent
South Africa 1900–1901

When the Boer War started in 1899, many young Australians made the decision to offer their services as soldiers. Many of them were to discover that getting into the various army units that were to head for South Africa wasn't as easy as they might have expected.

Cecil Ewens was determined to take part in the war as soon as he heard that the third contingent of South Australian troops, the South Australian Bushmen's Contingent, was to be formed. He caught the coach down to Adelaide from his home in Port Augusta and fronted up at the Exhibition Building where the recruiting office had been set up.

He joined a long line of hopefuls and watched in amazement as man after man was turned down without a word being said. He knew that only 14 more men were needed to reach the required complement of 100.

> After a certain amount of manoeuvring, I passed the different severe tests, unnecessarily so, without trouble, hundreds being turned away.

> While passing I might state that some splendid bushmen and fit for the greatest hardships were turned aside for some petty disfigurement while a few others with no bush experience were passed in.

> I entered the Exhibition Building in about the middle of a large number of men & filed along a rope. Took my hat off in the building, eventually it came my turn to be called over to the selectors, or waved on out as dozens had been before me.

> Looking across at the Bushmen's Judge & Jury, I was astounded to see the hand waving for me to pass on out without as much as a question. After having travelled

---

Trooper Cecil Ewens in uniform.

over 500 miles [800 km] in post haste to join this contingent, this reception was a stunner. In fact I was dumbfounded for the moment.

The hand kept on waving so out I went by the door at the rear. Gathering my thoughts together for a moment outside, I resolved to enter the building again by the front door. Entering, I found that the crowd of men had diminished considerably.

This time I kept my hat on & well over my eyes. The same performance was still going on waving them out with an odd one being called up now & again to be questioned etc.

My turn at last came again, this time I was called before the 'bench' without a demur and went through the rest of the performance without a hitch. The doctor examined my teeth as carefully as a horse dealer would an eight-year-old 'prad' at an auction sale.

Made to strip every vestige of clothing off, do a cake walk up & down the room in front of him, jab his finger here, jab his thumb there and eventually passed me out as sound & fit.

Cecil went into camp the next morning and just over a week later found himself on board the SS *Maplemore* heading out to sea. The voyage to South Africa was one to be remembered 'not for pleasure but with abhorrence and disgust'.

Fully 75 per cent of the food dealt out from the ships stores to the Troopers was simply scandalous; a tramp would not offer such food to a blackfella's dog in this country.

The salt pork was absolutely rotten and the unfortunate troopers who happened to be on fatigue duty had to go below and handle the putrid filth, long since recognised as pork.

Cecil wrote that the tea was undrinkable and the biscuits full of weevils. Naturally, complaints were made and the men were called on deck and given a lecture by the ship's captain, to the effect that they would thank their lucky stars if they fared so well in South Africa.

Once the troops had finally disembarked, they were concerned for the welfare of their horses. These were loaded onto trucks to travel several hundred kilometres in appalling conditions, with a number of them dying.

This was one of the many, many errors committed in South Africa during the war that came under my notice.

One of the first actions involving the South Australians occurred near Ottoshoop, not far from Mafeking.

> Left camp about 6 am, our Squadron being advance guard to the guns. Heard firing about 7 am, the Boers firing on the scouts. At 7.30 the guns began to play on the enemy. Shortly after that we were up to our neck in it, the enemy soon retired, our guns being too accurate.

> About 3.30 pm the New Zealanders, N.S. Wales, Victorians, Tasmanians and ourselves charged a string of *kopjes* [hills] at a hard gallop which we took in great style, the guns pouring in shells [all] the while.

> The Boers retired from their position in confusion but the country was very rugged here, they soon secured cover elsewhere. Saw three dead Boers during our charge.

A few days later they were in the thick of action again.

> Started out at 5 am to give the Boers a shaking up. Our column under Brigadier General Douglas on the left, another column under Lord Errol on the right—composed of NSW, Tasmanian and South Aus Bushmen, some Imperial Victorian B [Bushmen]. Our squadron had an important position as per usual, advance guard & scouts and started the ball rolling, our scouts being fired upon.

> We had four 15 pounders, 2 pompoms and some Maxims with us but they were not used during the day. We soon began to play upon them [the Boers] and they retired quickly. No damage done to our side.

> After hauling that lot of Boers, we went to some houses and burnt down the lot. Gave the women short notice to remove their goods. But a lot of different articles were burnt also.

> I was one of four tolled off to do the burning & of course we caught all the poultry handy. I felt rather sorry for the women but some Boers sniped at our patrol a few days before out of one of them.

> After doing this we advanced in extended order and drove the Boers back. They would not stand and have a shot at us. Captured 21 prisoners during the day, most of them were on foot and hid in the scrub, holes, trees etc.

Replacement horses, or remounts, were in constant demand but were generally snapped up by other units, much to the disgust of the South Australians who blamed their officers for not doing something about it.

The remounts arrived early and after the usual delay we made a start for the main camp, riding one & leading three horses apiece, 30 of us in charge of a Victorian Imperial Bushmen Lieutenant.

I picked a good horse, as I thought, out of the mob & rode him out. On arriving at the camp we were lined up and the staff picked out every good horse as they thought. We then took them over to the Imperial Yeomanry lines & exchanged these horses for theirs. I exchanged three then told them that the one I had saddled was one of their cast offs. Through this bit of manoeuvring I managed to stick to the remount I picked out in Ottoshoop.

This was another case of the many gross injustices that came under my notice during my term at the front. Our men without horses at this time had actually to take the sore-backed, badly knocked about horses that the Yeomanry had just exchanged away.

In September the squadron took part in a big battle.

About 11 am we were ordered to get our horses in & saddle up. Started out and were advancing in squadron column towards some *kopjes* about 3 miles [5 km] out that we knew the Boers occupied.

Got within 2000 yards [1800 m] when they began to pour the volleys in. We then dismounted and got behind cover and poured volleys into them. NSWB, NZ & Victorians were further along the ridge on our right, with big guns. Ten minutes later our squadron alone was ordered to charge a kopje across open country about half a mile [0.8 km] nearer the Boers. Directly the horses were brought up, the Boers turned most of their fire on them.

We mounted in double quick time, the bullets making one continual hiss the while. Our captain wanted us to dress up in line under this hail of bullets, but directly we heard what was wanted we let a yell out of us and charged across.

The big guns poured in shell and raked the kopjes. Luckily only one horse was killed, two others wounded. The owner of the horse that was killed had to run the last two hundred yards for shelter under the kopje.

We took up a position on the kopje and began returning the Boers fire which was very warm. About quarter of an hour afterwards we got the order to retire again much to our disgust.

We galloped back again all scattered out in a terrific hail of bullets. My *beautiful mount* went dead lame on me again. I was one of the first to make the charge on the kopje but was quite 200 yards [180 m] behind when the others reached it. In the retirement I simply cantered back and was very little further than halfway when the others pulled up.

No mistake, the bullets did kick up a din, our own forces firing over my head and the Boers keeping up an incessant fire from behind. One hundred packets of crackers going off near your ear at once would be only a mild comparison.

In mid-December the squadron was near Lichtenburg.

Had hardly got into bed when we were ordered out again at 12 o'clock. Started out at 1.30 am and picked the Boers up at sunrise but they were not speaking and went for all they were worth.

Colonel Merritt went out in a slightly different direction with a portion of the mounted men. Of course we started after the Boers, our regiment going out on the right flank. We galloped for about seven miles [11 km] before we caught up to part of the convoy, 8 waggons & some scotch carts all loaded with different stuff. Unfortunately our squadron was on the left flank so were not in the waggon catching, although we got plenty of stock.

We then halted for about two hours, then started to return bringing in 1000 head of cattle & the same number of sheep.

On Christmas Day the cook made some plum puddings.

I believe the officers gave some silver to put in them. The puddings turned out very well and I managed to find sixpence in my slice. Had a spell in the afternoon after a very rough week.

But the rest didn't last long. At 2.30 am on Boxing Day they were called out again and chased a group of Boers, who managed to escape into the bush.

Despite expecting to be sent home at any time, the squadron continued to be involved in the fighting. While at Mafeking on 23 January 1901, they heard of the death of Queen Victoria.

Cecil's diary ends on 26 January 1901.

The war over, he returned to Australia. After marrying Emily, he worked on Bungaree Station about 160 km north of Adelaide in South Australia where their five children were born. They later moved to Caroona Station about 50 km further north. Cecil Ewens died in 1944.

Supplied by Robert Ewens of South Australia

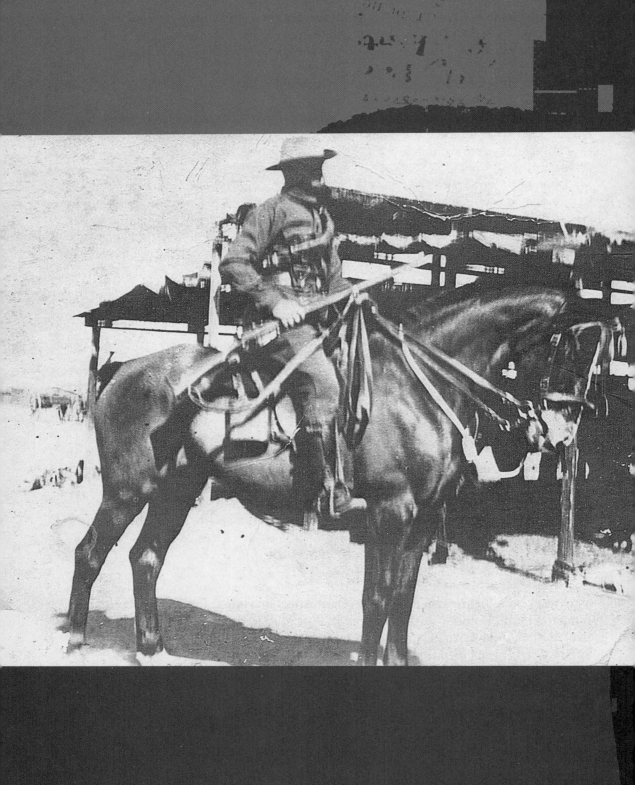

Charles Haslett
Civilian Dispatch Rider and News Agent
Natal Field Force
South Africa 1900

T hings were tough in Australia in the 1890s with little work available in the building trade. Faced with a number of debts, Charles Alexander Haslett decided to leave his home in Sorrento, Victoria, and try his luck in South Africa, where he planned to make a fresh start.

His timing was unfortunate, for he arrived in South Africa with his wife, Dora, and their baby son, Alexander, just before the start of the Boer War.

Soon after war was declared, Dora and Alexander returned to Sorrento, while Charles remained in South Africa. He had little success in the building trade but, as he had some experience as a photographer and journalist, he decided to travel with the troops working as a despatch rider and news agent to the Natal Field Force.

Writing to his father in April 1900, Charles Haslett had obviously had enough of the fighting and described some of the action he had seen.

> I am awfully sick of this life, it is a dogs life but I had no choice. The Building trade was bad. All works were stopped directly the War started. However I have seen something to talk and think of to the end of my days. I have seen every fight for the relief of Ladismith. Our big guns fired on the Boer positions for three days. On the Third we advanced and the Boers let some of our men get up within 200 yards [180 m] before a shot was fired then it was awfull, the Bullets hissed and pinged everywhere and the large shells Screaming overhead. It was simply Hell let Loose however I did not get hit. God only knows.

Charles Haslett in uniform mounted on his horse.

Since Colenso day I have been very careful not to get in to Rifle Range the shell fire is not so dangerous. I have been under shell fire several times since. As well as Colenso I have seen the Battle of Spion Kop, Potgieters Drift, Hussar Hill. This was a very funny affair when the Boers saw our men approaching to them they made off and left their German Officer having breakfast. He made a lot of fuss about being neutral and all the rest of it but on being searched only two revolvers and a murderous looking knife was found on him. I tried hard to get the knife but while we were parlaying an Officer came up and he lost the lot.

Well then the next fight was from Hussar Hill with all the big guns directed on Hlanwani but when our men advanced the Boers Bolted again then Buller crossed the Zugela for the fourth time. Well he gave them such a bad time on Groblers Kloof and the surrounding hills they fell back onto Monte Christo. Then Buller had to cross back over the Zugela and work back around Hlanwani and they drove them all along Monte Christo right back to Pieters. There he had them in a terrible plight and simply Murdered them. The first thing in the morning they hoisted the white flag, our fellows stopped firing. And about fifteen men and an Officer went to take them prisoners. When they got about 10 yds [9 m] off The Boers fired killed & wounded the lot. When Buller heard of this he saw no more white Flags. Although they were popping up any where that it was a bit hot.

The sights I saw on Pieters Hill after the fight I will never forget. I tried to Photograph it but was prevented by an Officer. The trench they had dug to fight in they were buried in. Our men just straightened them lengthwise and covered. No one knows who is buried like this. Well in that trench alone I could count 123 Boers and Germans, English and Irish all fighting against us. That is only one trench of a dozen similar. They have even tied their dead together and tied a weight on them and thrown them in the river (Zugela). Of course they have come up and our people have had to bury them. That was their last stand at Pieters. They Bolted through the night and left a clear road into Ladismith.

If you could only see the positions from Colenso to Ladismith the whole world would never get the British out of (never). The Boers are arrant cowards, they are very good at setting traps but they take very good care that they are 20 to 1 if they come out into the open. Another thing they are very fond of doing is to find out where an outpost is stationed and perhaps a couple of old Boers Snipers will sneak down and shoot all night at anything that shows itself. Now our men go to a certain place in the daylight and directly it gets dark they move further in or away.

One night last week at Sundays River a very good thing was done by one fellow in outpost. Two Boers had sneaked down for some sport. Well some of our Maxim Guns are very lightly made and one of our outposts had been allowed to take this with them so when it got dark nothing could move on our side of the river but crack would go a rifle. Our fellows were determined to bag these fellows so they slipped half way down hill with this Maxim and the fellows on top of the hill kept these amused till just the peep of daylight. Then these two got up to dip back and they played this Maxim on them. Bear in mind the Maxim fires 300 shots a minute anyway when they went for those two Boers they were simply riddled. Well those two with the Maxim instead of being praised they were scolded for going beyond the picket. The Army is simply rotten with red Tape. If they would only give our fellows a free hand Mr Boer would not be so cheeky but so far the Boers have Bluffed Tommy Atkins something awful.

I am at Elandslaagte just now. Last Tuesday & Wednesday I suppose you may have got it in the papers by now they started quite unawares and gave us a good old shelling. You could not move from them. We had 3 killed and about 6 wounded and lost several horses. I was driving through the camp with my papers when they started but I kept on and came out alright. One poor chap lying in his tent got his arm carried away. I have not heard how he is getting on. The Boers have shifted back again so I don't expect we will see much more fighting from this side. I think this war will have a very sudden end. It is rumoured in Camp that Kruger [the Boer leader] himself is shot. How true it is I cannot tell. However before this reaches you there will be some big thing happen.

I will tell you a little about myself. I have had a very bad time the last month, first the Fever then a cold and a relapse which nearly settled me. I laid in my tent with nothing but a Bottle of Enos fruit Salts for four days, then my mate came and he got me some quinine and I shook the fever off but I caught a very bad cold and had a relapse—even now if I cross the tent I perspire awfull. I have to change my Shirts every

The White House at Sorrento, built by Charles Haslett. It was later burnt down.

9

morning yet if you saw me just now you would never know me. I have a beard of four weeks growth and my face is all pinched up and my eyes right back in my head. I can tell you I do look a beauty. Some of the soldiers that knew me before ask me all sorts of Questions such as walking about to save funeral expenses and such like. I ate nothing whatever for three weeks just a cup of Bovril now & then.

I have been punished out here but I thought there was the chance of getting square with all so I have done my best. Oh I nearly forgot to mention Dora tells me in letter that her Mother has cleared the ground for her. That will be so much off your shoulders too. I will do my very best to clear A Kerr & Co liability. I think I will do a good thing in Sorrento one way and another and hope to repay you for all the worry I have caused you. I hope to leave here in three months at the most. Remember me to Mother and all at home, hoping to see you all and in good health very soon.

Charles Haslett survived the war despite the ravages of fever. In fact, more Australians died of disease during the war than were killed by Boer bullets.

On his return to Australia, he was reunited with Dora and Alexander and went on to build a guest house at Sorrento. He gave a number of public talks about his experiences in South Africa, including one at Collingwood Town Hall on 23 August 1900 at which he recounted his experiences of battles, illustrated by 100 Limelight Views [lantern slides]. Admission was sixpence and one shilling. The show concluded with the singing of patriotic songs.

Dora died when she was only 43 and Charles remarried. He had four more children with his second wife, two sons and two daughters.

Supplied by Marjorie Whitbourne [née Haslett] of Victoria

COLLINGWOOD TOWN HALL.

THURSDAY, AUGUST 23, 1900,

Charles HASLETT

Despatch Rider and News Agent to the Natal Field Forces,

WILL RELATE HIS

SEVEN MONTHS' EXPERIENCES

WITH THE TROOPS UNDER

General Buller.

EYE-WITNESS OF BATTLES AT

Elands=Laagte. Colenso. Spion Kop. Vaal Krantz.
Railway Hill. Pieter's Hill. Relief of Ladysmith.

Illustrated by 100 *LIMELIGHT VIEWS.*

Cinematographe *by J. YEOMANS.*

Vocalists—Mr. W. G. BARKER and Mr. ARNOLD,

PATRIOTIC SONGS.

Admission = 6d. and 1s.

DOORS OPEN 7-30.
COMMENCE AT 8.

G. F. COLLIS, PRINTER, 345 VICTORIA STREET, ABBOTSFORD.

'THE FIRST AUSTRALIAN TO FALL IN ACTION IN S.A.'

Private Victor Jones
1st Queensland Mounted Infantry
South Africa 1900

P rivate Victor Jones of 1st Queensland Mounted Infantry, the first Queensland contingent, was the first Australian to die in action in the Boer War when he was killed in an ambush on 1 January 1900.

His death led to an extraordinary exchange of letters that are held in the National Archives of Australia. It culminated 100 years later with a wreath-laying ceremony on Jones' grave at Sunnyside, near Salt Lake, north of Cape Town.

Victor Jones was an employee of the Mount Morgan Company in Queensland when the Boer War broke out. He had worked his way up from office boy 'to one of considerable responsibility' according to an article in the *Queenslander Illustrated Supplement*.

His brother, G B Jones, who worked for the Railway Department at Rockhampton, described his brother as 'a very fine young man, aged 27, 6ft in height, who at the first announcement of sending a Queensland contingent to South Africa gave up a good position, home & friends to fight for his Queen and country.'

According to G B Jones, his brother was in the first scouting party of four men, under Lieutenant A G Adie, who were sent out on the morning of the Sunnyside engagement. He was shot dead on the veldt when his group were surprised by about 14 Boers.

A second Queenslander, Private David Cumming McLeod of Toowong, was wounded in action later that day and died some hours later. Both men were buried where they were killed, about 1.5 km apart from each other.

Thanks to the compassion and persistence of members of the Guild of Loyal Women of South Africa, the graves of the two men were subsequently located and marked.

Private Victor Jones in uniform.

A Miss Charlotte C Slater, a member of the guild, wrote to the Governor of Queensland in September 1901 in a bid to locate the nearest relatives of the two men so she could ascertain if they wished to have anything done in regard to the graves.

Her letter was forwarded to G B Jones who responded to Miss Slater expressing his family's gratitude for 'taking such an interest in the grave of our loved one (which) is the source of the greatest consolation and thankfulness to us.'

Jones asked for a headstone with stone kerbing to be erected on the grave, and with the words, 'In loving memory of Trooper Victor S. Jones Q.M.I of Rockhampton, Queensland, Killed January 1st 1900 aged 27 years. The first Australian to fall in action in S.A.' He offered to help pay for the headstone.

A year later, Miss Lilian Orpen, honorary secretary of the guild's branch at St Clair, Douglas, wrote to the Queensland Governor stating that she had heard nothing more from Mr Jones since he had written requesting the erection of a headstone. She said she had also written to McLeod's family but had received no reply.

Miss Orpen said she had collected £30-5-0 from the Loyalists of Douglas to erect the headstone and railing around the graves, but had been prevented from beginning work at the graves due to the disturbed state of the country.

She went on to say, 'But as soon as Peace was declared I ordered a stone and railing for Trooper Jones grave and should the funds prove sufficient I shall order the same for the grave of Trooper McLeod.'

This prompted a letter in December 1902 from G B Jones to the Governor's Office expressing regret for not replying, as he had been in a serious accident that had incapacitated him for many months. He stated he had written to Miss Orpen by the same mail, enclosing 'a postal order for £10 from my sisters and myself towards the cost of the stone and railing and thanking her very sincerely for her great kindness in the matter.'

And that might have concluded the affair but for the actions of the present owners of nearby Sunnydale Farm, Jean and Herbert Dugmore, who, in late 1999, contacted Trooper Jones' great-niece, Fiona Bekkers of Ascot in Brisbane. They invited her to take part in a wreath-laying ceremony at the grave on 1 January 2000, 100 years to the day Trooper Jones was killed. Mrs Bekkers accepted the invitation and wrote the following description of the ceremony.

> The ceremony at the graveside on 1/1/2000 commenced at 9 am when it was already very hot. There were about 40 people there including the Dugmore family, who arranged the whole thing, and other neighbouring (mainly Afrikaans) farmers and nine Queenslanders (six reserve members of 2/14 QMI [2nd/14th Light

Horse Regiment (QMI) Association], my husband, son and myself). The service was conducted by Ken Dugmore, son of Jean and Herbert, our hosts, and opened with a prayer. Pieter Pieterse spoke next on behalf of the Boers, describing events leading to the war and its aftermath, including the benefits. I spoke next, mainly on a personal note about Great Uncle Victor, and laid a wreath at the newly re-erected headstone followed by the QMI soldiers who each laid a poppy. Wreaths were also laid at the communal grave marked by stones where lay the remains of the seven unknown Boers who died that day.

Taped national anthems were provided by the soldiers who carried flags and formed a guard, while the Last Post was played by a local black student. Many blacks on both sides were also victims of the war. Then we all climbed to the Sunnyside Memorial on top of the nearby kopje where I helped unveil the plaque. A local historian gave a good description of the action that day 100 years ago, pointing out the landmarks to us as he spoke. After this we all were ready for brunch under the tarpaulin at the bottom of the hill. Afternoon tea was provided at the nearby Fort Richmond, built by the British troops during the Boer War.

Supplied by Fiona Bekkers of Queensland

'COME ON AUSTRALIANS, SHOW THESE FRENCH AND BRITISH BEGGARS HOW TO FIGHT'

Private Gordon Craig
6th Battalion, Australian Imperial Force
Egypt and Gallipoli 1915

T he many harrowing accounts of the landing at Gallipoli give substance to the horrors faced by the Anzacs as they headed for the beach in boats and while they were fighting their way up the steep inclines against appalling odds.

Private Harold Gordon Craig survived the early fighting but was wounded and evacuated to Cairo. He described the landing in a letter to his brother Ken, written from his hospital bed on 18 May 1915.

He wrote how his wounds were mending and that he expected to be fit again in a couple of weeks and would then go back to the front.

I shall be jolly glad when I do go, but hope it won't be as bad as before.

He explained how, when in Egypt, the troops were given orders to get their kit ready. They were given 50 rounds of ammunition each, which took the weight of their packs to almost 68 kg.

They then marched more than 19 km to Cairo and caught the train for Alexandria, arriving the next morning. They boarded ships immediately and sailed for Lemnos, where they stayed for two weeks awaiting the arrival of more troops.

Well, we received a letter from Lord Kitchener telling us that we were going to do work that no soldiers had ever been asked to do before, and that it would go down in history and a lot more as to the Colonials. Told us that we would have a very hard time as we would land under fire. Never tumbled that it would be so bad as it was.

Private Gordon Craig in uniform.

One night about 12 we sailed from where we were, about 4 am I heard a gun burst over my head, so went down below—wasn't taking any risks. We had breakfast and then started to disembark.

There were about four destroyers firing on the Turks, *Queen Elizabeth,* the *London* and don't know what the other two were. A Company was the first to land then B and C. I was looking out of the port hole and could see about a million Turks on the beach and cliffs banging away at our boys for all they were worth.

We had to climb down the ship rope ladder into our boat. There were about 10 boats and 25 men in each boat. A tug took us within 100 yards of the beach and we had to row the rest of the way. The shrapnel was bursting all round us, also machine guns, rifle shot.

We lost a lot of men before we landed, but our boat got ashore safely. The Naval Officer in our boat—a big fat chap—when a shrapnel burst within a yard of us laughed and said 'Oh never mind them, the beggars couldn't hit a hay stack.'

I believe the first lot to arrive fixed bayonets in the water and did not wait for any orders but simply charged the Turks. Some of them dropped the guns and cried for mercy, which they didn't get, and the rest went for their lives to the trenches.

Well we landed. We marched about 100 yards and then took a rest and then word came to go up into the firing line at once. We threw our packs away and then got on with the game. The country was so rough and scrubby that you couldn't see where you were going and the shrapnel was bursting all round us and the bullets were so thick that we thought they were bees buzzing about us.

I was hiding behind a bush and the bullets were cutting the leaves off. There must have been 100,000 Turks against 20,000 Australians as the French and British landed somewhere else so you can see we were having a pretty hot time, especially as we did not have artillery with us.

By this time we were all mixed up with different Companies and I heard one of our officers call out 'Are there any men about here?' So I called out that I was there. So we advanced together. We came to a gully and laid there for a rest. The shrapnel was worse than hell, was getting nearer to us every minute, so I said to the officer that we ought to get into the firing line and try and pot a few Turks before we throw a seven. The rotten beggar wasn't having any so I left him.

Then I got up to the firing line. I was lying next to a major who was shot in both legs. He asked me what sort of shot I was so I told him not bad, so told me to try the range at 500 yards, but my shot went over their heads so tried 450 and got right on to them. It was awful hearing the wounded crying out and seeing the dead lying round you.

Well after a while a bullet hit me, and just grazed my wrist enough to burn the skin. I didn't take any notice of that, but about five minutes after one got me clean through the arm. I tried to go on but was settled. Just as I got hit the chap next to me got one also.

I then made my way back to the beach. I reckon I have more luck than Jessie the Elephant not getting hit on the way back. When I got back the doctor dressed my wounds. I went into the hospital boat. We lost 15 men on the boat. There were about 5,000 to 6,000 wounded and killed the first day.

Private Craig went on to recount reports he had heard that, after he was evacuated from Gallipoli, the 2nd Brigade, of which the 6th Battalion was a part, had been sent to reinforce the French and British at Cape Helles after two days' rest and with barely 1000 men left.

They were told that as they put in such good work the first day that it was a post of honour they were being sent there.

When they arrived I believe it was as bad as when we landed. The French are fair squibs, worse than Ricketts. Our boys advanced to where the French and British were.

The brigadier came along and called out, 'Come on Australians, show these French and British beggars how to fight.' That was enough. They jumped out of the trenches and charged. They left the French and British behind but the Australians got shot down like rabbits. I believe there is only about 200 of the 2nd Brigade left on the field and not one officer.

Well Ken, I suppose you are tired of reading this and think I am boasting of ourselves too much but everybody calls us the 'White Gurkhas'. A Tommy told me that a Seat of Gold was not good enough for the Australians to sit upon. When you receive this I will be right in it again.

Gordon Craig was sent back to Gallipoli where he was severely wounded by an exploding bomb during an attack on the German officers' trench on 7 August. He died the next day, 8 August 1915, on the hospital ship *Dunluce Castle* and was buried at sea.

He is commemorated at the Lone Pine Memorial at Gallipoli, which is dedicated to 'the glory of God and in lasting memorial of 3268 Australian soldiers who fought on Gallipoli in 1915 and have no known graves, and 456 New Zealand soldiers whose names are not recorded in other areas of the Peninsula but who fell in the Anzac area and have no known graves; and also of 960 Australians and 252 New Zealanders who, fighting on Gallipoli in 1915, incurred mortal wounds or sickness and found burial at sea.'

Supplied by Colin Melville of Victoria

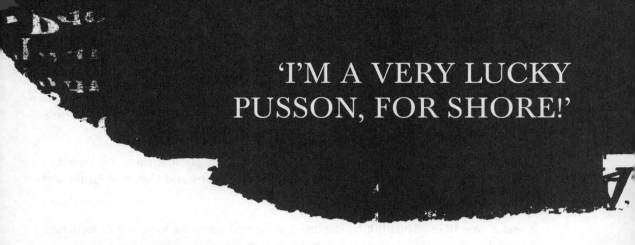

'I'M A VERY LUCKY PUSSON, FOR SHORE!'

Captain John Lawrence Whitham
12th Battalion, Australian Imperial Force
Gallipoli 1915

Laurie Whitham, a professional soldier, had reason to remember 25 April 1915. He was at Gallipoli and was 'lucky' to get a wound that was serious enough to take him out of the firing line without being life-threatening.

When he wrote to his parents from Deaconess's Hospital in Alexandria, he was in good spirits but mindful of the events that had recently taken place.

> Though our casualties were heavy, it could not be expected otherwise. And what is most important, our task was done. Twas a close go, but if the few items we have seen so far in the papers—the cables here are not extensive—about the congratulatory messages from London to Australia are correct—the results must have been satisfactory and April 25th is a day to be remembered—also the 26th and several other days.

As the commanding officer of C Company, 12th Battalion, Captain Whitlam was in the thick of things during the landing and the subsequent fighting throughout the first two days. Although he landed with the company, within a short time everyone was mixed up with other units.

> During one burst of shell fire I got a bump in the left arm—just sufficiently hard enough to make you think some practical joker had hit you with a poker or a ruler on the biceps! That's what the feeling was like: only a wee bit of blood came out of the hole in the jacket sleeve, so that was alright.

> I didn't have to make tracks for the base at the beach as I would have had the bit of lead come about three inches [75 mm] to the right. The shoulder strap of my web equipment (officers all wear the same equipment as men) was punctured first and probably diverted the bullet into the arm.

Captain John Lawrence Witham in uniform.

21

I was lying down using my glasses when hit—good job it didn't hit the glasses or I'd have had to get a new pair, and perhaps a new face also!

Captain Whitham kept fighting, rounding up his stray troops and digging in for the night.

About 6 pm I found a corporal and about six men of my company and we joined in digging in a line; found Rafferty also about this time and he and Corporal Austin and myself passed the night in one hole together.

It was a wee hole at first but by daybreak it formed part of a long line of trenches. Am afraid I didn't do much of the digging though.

Here I've gone rambling on—almost started to tell you about the sights and sounds but they are not for letters home, and such things can be better described by newspaper correspondents—or told when the war is over when people want to hear something gruesome.

But one must just say one word about the way those lads took their punishment. Badly wounded, horribly wounded, men would stick it all with hardly a murmur. And there was not much in the way of attention for them for the first 24 hours. The stretcher bearers and ambulance men were just splendid, but their work was heavy and they had many casualties themselves.

Laurie Whitham was sent down to the beach to have his dressing treated but was told he would have to go out to one of the hospital ships to have the bullet taken out. He eventually ended up in hospital at Alexandria.

Here I am back in Egypt just two months after leaving it—sounds like Rudyard Kipling in *Mandalay* doesn't it? But it wasn't a fondness for Egypt which brought me back to it, altho' I'm having an or'fly good time here all the same.

I've found that if a fellow is looking for a nice easy job with nice people, he can't do better than get a slight wound (a sprained ankle will do as well as any other) but say, for preference, a puncture of the arm—left arm, of course. It will ensure him a pleasant sea voyage, a transference from ship to a nice hospital in a nice springy motor car ambulance, a comfy bed in a nice bright room which opens on to a fine roomy balcony two stories above the ground.

Being careful not to upset the censors, Laurie Whitham then described events leading up to the landing and his eventual wounding.

I told you in previous letters from our late resting place that a Big Ball was expected to take place soon and that we, our Brigade, had secured 'early door tickets'. We were the covering party for the Division, or rather for our Army Corps, because units of both divisions landed during that day and the next.

Just before dawn the first boats reached the beach. These contained two companies from each of the 9th, 10th and 11th Battalions; the remaining 6 Coys and the 4 Coys of the 12th following in quick succession.

The first men ashore rushed the first steep hill in front, under fire, and cleared the first ridge with the bayonet. The fire increased every minute, rifles, machine guns and shrapnel, plenty of poor fellows never reached the shore. Col Hawley, [Lieutenant-Colonel Sydney Hawley, second-in-command of the 12th Battalion] I believe, got hit badly before he left the deck of the torpedo boat.

There was no time for anything but hurried rallies of each company as they landed—then a dash and scramble forward up hills and down gullies—such hills and gullies they were too; very steep, and mainly covered with a low scrub, which, although it afforded excellent cover from view for the defenders, was not much use in that way for us.

Our lines gradually spread out in a semi-circle. The flanks towards the coast and the centre pushed forward. Other brigades of our division soon reinforced us, and we kept pushing forward, units, companies and battalions getting mixed up, despite all efforts to keep them complete and separate. 'Twas quite unavoidable and by nightfall it was quite common to see men of different brigades lying alongside of each other, and lines of rapidly constructed trenches occupied by very much mixed up units, each little group taking orders from the nearest officer of NCO.

From daylight to nightfall we enjoyed the attentions of our friends the enemy, and as they were all so well concealed and knew the ranges so exactly, it was not surprising that they were able to give us such a hot time. And it was a hot time.

The behaviour of the lads was just splendid, even when their leaders were gone they kept well to the front, and despite their losses, never lost heart. There were times when portions of the line had to fall back, having gone, perhaps, too far forward, or having met with close range fire from concealed rifles and machine guns, but they were always ready to rally.

Captain Whitham described the tremendous noise from the guns fired from ships off Anzac Cove and then from the howitzers as they were manhandled ashore and hauled up the ridges from the beach.

There would be a rushing, hustling railway noise in the air, then a terrific cloud of smoke, followed often by several other similar rushing, hustling noises and more clouds of smoke. Then came the bang-bang; first the bang-bang-bang from the sea—then the bung whooff-bung whoo-off-bung from the shore.

Lordy, I didn't envy the gentlemen in those redoubts and field works, well dug in though they may have been.

Our own little Battalion (and it is a little one now, how strong actually I can't say) got its share of casualties. Out of 28 officers who landed on the 25th, only 8 were available for duty on Monday afternoon. There may have been further casualties since—5 were killed outright and 15 wounded—more or less severely—most of us, however, will soon be fit for the front again.

All we can be thankful for as father would say 'That it was no wuss'—for there's no reason whatever that each wounded man was not a dead man—only the little Cherub that looks after soldiers and sailors can say why there were not more fatal lists. I know I'm quite satisfied with my own little lot. I'm a very lucky pusson, for shore! And I just guess as how my good luck will stick to me.

Captain Whitham's luck did hold. He survived Gallipoli, being Mentioned in Despatches and made a Companion of the Order of St Michael and St George (CMG). He spent a further three years on the Western Front, where he commanded the 52nd Battalion and then the 49th Battalion, twice more being Mentioned in Despatches. He was also awarded the Distinguished Service Order for action at Villers-Bretonneux. He returned to Australia and remained in the Army, eventually reaching the rank of Lieutenant-General in command of Southern Command early in World War II. He retired in 1941 but was recalled as Officer-in-Charge of the Volunteer Defence Corps (VDC).

Supplied by Marie Kays of Tasmania

Painting of John Lawrence Whitham CMG DSO, c 1944.

'AN ABOMINABLE ITCH'

Second Lieutenant Frank Boyes
14th Battalion, Australian Imperial Force
Gallipoli 1915

 he sight of Australian diggers walking naked up the beach at Gallipoli would have caused great amusement had it not been for the seriousness of the situation. It must have had the Turks wondering what was going on, too.

Frank Boyes explained this strange event after the war.

> We landed on Gallipoli in what we were wearing and continued to wear it day and night until the socks were the first garments to become unwearable, and they were cast out and we went barefoot in our boots.

> We discarded our tunics during the day as the weather became hotter, and working and living in earthen trenches, while sometimes sweating profusely caused our pants and thick pure woollen shirts to become even worse than filthy.

> We got only sufficient fresh water, in fact, on some days barely enough to drink, so washing garments was out of the question, and so the only alternative was to get down to the beach and wash our garments and ourselves in the brine, which as far as our garments wars concerned made little difference.

Lieutenant Boyes said their turn for the beach trip occurred about once in 10 or 14 days.

> The Turks had a battery of guns, each of which we called 'Beachy Bill', which could land shells on any given spot of more than half a dozen men congregated for more than a few seconds. So, it might happen that one's trip to the beach was a 'washout'.

When the men reached the water's edge, they hastily undressed and then washed and wrung out their pants, shirts and other garments and spread them out on the shingle while they washed or indulged in a swim. Not having time to let their

Second Lieutenant Frank Boyes in uniform.

clothes dry properly because of the Turkish shelling and objecting to wearing wet clothes, they would put on their hats and boots and start off back up to the trenches, swinging a shirt in one hand and pants in the other to help them dry as quickly as possible.

It was a man's world as there were no women or children within our boundaries to be considered and the Officers right up through to General Birdwood himself did not seem to worry about our dress or undress so long as we could and would fight the enemy when necessary.

But, the sight of those men (I did it too) clad only in boots and hat walking back from the beach swinging their pants and shorts is a sight I have never forgotten.

Another sight never to be forgotten was to see men—naked or partly clad—seated in the sun with a garment spread over their knees, pressing intently at the seams on the inside. This was known as 'chatting' and, for some, it was an almost daily occurrence.

There were parasites which caused an abominable itch to whichever part of the skin where they operated. They lived and bred mainly in the seams of the inner garments and as there was no hot water or chemicals available for their control or destruction the field was open for them to multiply and flourish. The best control means available was to wear the clothing inside out and then there were no seams next to the skin for the pest to hide away in and breed. This I did with my flannel shirt, but I simply could not come at wearing my trousers inside out, even though many of the other men did. It simply looked too awful.

Lieutenant Boyes said that immersing the clothing in the seawater made no difference. Indeed, some men declared that it gave the pest increased vitality. When the troops left Gallipoli and went to France, there were facilities for washing and fumigating the clothing, which made life more liveable. If silk or some such material was worn next to the skin there was no irritation.

We veterans of the lst War were unanimous in declaring that the chats on Gallipoli were harder to endure than all the Turks, tucker and all the other conditions combined.

Supplied by Lyn Skyba of Victoria

The beach at Gallipoli.

KOPS

ANZAC

HONOR TO THE LIVING

HMS QUEEN ELIZABETH

GALLIPOLI

IMMORTAL GLORY TO THE DEAD

TOAST

BRISBANE

MUIRS LTD

PROTECTING THE NAME OF ANZAC

Crown Solicitor's Office
Civilian
Melbourne, Victoria

 Even before Australian troops had left Gallipoli, people had come to realise the value of the term 'Anzac'.

But when those in business began trying to capitalise on it by using it to promote their products, the Commonwealth Government swiftly introduced the *War Precautions Act 1914–1916*, which outlawed this practice without special permission.

The Commonwealth Attorney-General administered the Act and the Crown Solicitor's office was given the task of monitoring the use of the term and carrying out prosecutions to discourage those who sought to benefit illegally from featuring it.

A typical example was the Anzac Golliwog Company that provided variety entertainment around the traps. A man calling himself Driver H N Walker headed the company. He performed with his 'famous dog Anzac'. On his playbill, Walker claimed to have seen 858 days of active service, and to be someone who has 'performed before Royalty and who has been decorated by Queen Alexandra.'

His supporting cast included Bert's Canine Comedy Co (a clever troupe of performing dogs, including Miss Pearl, who dived from a ladder 8 metres high), Drewy the juggling drum major and the Golliwog Costume Comedy Company.

Its cast included 'Miss Kitty Renby, impersonater [sic], Miss Irene Harrison, Mr John Walker, baritone, Mr Geo Drew, monologist, Mr Jack Herbert, comedian, in duets, trios, concerted items and comedy burlesques.'

Anzac Toast beer labels were rejected by the Crown's Solicitor's Office.

Walker was interview by Police Sergeant Kersley at Albury, after the Anzac Golliwog Company had performed at the Mechanics' Theatre on Tuesday 21 August 1917. Sergeant Kersley sent his report to the Superintendent of Police, who in turn submitted it to the Inspector-General of Police in Sydney.

In his statement to police, Walker said he had taken his dog with him when he left Australia on 14 October 1915 to fight at Gallipoli. The dog also accompanied him to France and then back to Australia in October 1916.

> I was discharged on 28 December 1916. In February this year [1917] I started under engagement to Hugh Macintosh at the Tivoli Theatre to show the 'Dog Anzac'. Since then I worked in Melbourne and suburbs till 7 July. I then started to travel with the dog and show him at various theatres and later on formed the company known as 'Anzac Gollywog Co'. I am the owner of the company. Mr Drew manages for me.

> I have no written authority to use the word 'Anzac' in connection with dog or with the Company. I got permission in London from the War Office to allow my dog to retain the name 'Anzac'. It was not in writing.

The report was forwarded to the Commonwealth Attorney-General's office and was reviewed by Army Intelligence before prosecution was recommended. But by then Walker had moved on and was back in Melbourne. Some discussion ensued about whether to proceed with the charges in Melbourne or in Albury where the offence was committed.

Eventually, the Crown Solicitor wrote to the Secretary of the Attorney-General's Department outlining events to date.

I think that the intention of Sub-section 4 of Section 6 was that a prosecution could be instituted in any place where the defendant was found at the time the proceedings were instituted but I think that difficulties may be met with if it is attempted to prosecute in Melbourne, because if it is alleged in the Information that the offence was committed in Albury, the Court may, in spite of the Section, decline to entertain jurisdiction, and if it is alleged that the offence was committed in Melbourne, the evidence in support of the charge will show that it was committed in Albury in another State.

The offence does not appear to have been a very serious one, and if proceedings were instituted in Albury, the defendant would necessarily be put to considerable expense in attending the trial.

The defendant was interviewed by Police at Albury in respect of the matter of his use of the word 'Anzac' and he apparently gave a frank account of how he came to use the word, and I think it is probable that when he came to know that he was contravening the Regulations he discontinued the use of the word 'Anzac' as part of the name of his Company.

Under the circumstances it might be desirable to inquire further into the matter before proceeding with prosecution.

It can be assumed that prosecution of Driver H N Walker did not proceed, but many others did. Once the Act came into force, many individuals and businesses that had already begun using the term in various ways sought permission to continue to do so. Many had gone to some expense in printing stationery or having signs made. Others wanted to immortalise loved ones who had been killed in the war by naming their homes Anzac. But even Gallipoli veterans were prevented from doing this.

Mrs Agnes Fowles wrote to obtain permission to continue calling her private residence 'Anzac'. She said the house had been given to her by her late son Sergeant H Fowles, who had served with the 9th Battalion and had died leading his men at the Gallipoli landing.

I named the house 'Anzac' in honour of his memory. My husband, Maj J K Fowles, has also given military service both in the Sth African campaign and in the present war.

Her request was refused.

A refusal was also received by Mr R H Burton who wanted to name his private residence after his late brother, Corporal Alexander Stewart Burton VC, who was killed at Lone Pine on Gallipoli in the action for which he was awarded the Victoria Cross.

Some even wished to give the name to a son. Mr Thomas Edward Drane, late of the 1st Field Company Engineers, wrote asking for permission to call his son George Anzac.

The reason I ask you is this to be sure that it is legal for an original Anzac to name his child as above.

I myself left Australia with the First Div in October 1914 and I was wounded in Gallipoli, which cost me a leg. Also I was the first to volunteer from this Town [Forbes] and my child is the first to be born here with an Anzac for his father.

My wife's brother also left with the First Div and he laid down his life at Gallipoli and that is the reason we want to name him so. Hoping to here very favourably from you.

Mr Drane was advised there was no legal objection to use of the name Anzac in the naming of children.

When the Kops Brewery in Queensland sought permission to print beer labels called Anzac Toast, they were refused. On the other hand, Private Harold Walter Cavill, who enlisted in the 2nd Battalion AIF on 24 August 1914 (enlistment began on 10 August 1914), had his application for copyright of a postcard featuring a wounded digger and the words 'Jolly Good Luck in the New Year, My Old Dinkum Anzac', approved.

Private Cavill was repatriated to Australia in July 1915, so was probably wounded at Gallipoli. The Dinkum Anzac from his postcard was also featured on the cover of his book, *Imperishable Anzacs: A Story of Australia's 1st Brigade*, which was based on his diary and published in 1916.

Mr W E Perry of Wallaroo in South Australia wrote to the Minister for Defence, Senator George Pearce, seeking permission to retain the word Anzac painted on the front of his billiard saloon, hair dressing and tobacconist business.

Some time ago I had the word 'Anzac' placed over the saloon, mostly in honour of over one hundred of my customers who has enlisted and seen service both at Gallipolli and now many are in France. Some of them Sir has laid down their life and will never return. Many has been wounded and ill whilst others so far has been lucky enough to pull through, so far, without being injured at all.

Mr Perry was disappointed.

Music publishers generally had better luck. *The Anzac (The bravest thing God ever made)*, a stirring march with words by Will H Ogilvie and music by Miss May Summerbelle, was approved.

The promoter, J C Williamson, had the cover of his songbook, *The House That Jack Built*, featuring patriotic songs, approved. The managing director of Allen & Co Pty Ltd cited this as an example while seeking approval for his album of dance music, *Songs of Anzac*. He also gained permission.

Written by Tony Miller from information supplied
by the National Archives of Australia, Canberra, ACT

Mr Perry's ill-fated Anzac Billiard Palace.

9. 4th L.H. of A.I.F. Shoeing an outlaw in the desert of Egypt.

THE WAR IN THE DESERT ON HORSEBACK

Farrier Sergeant Harold Mertin
9th Light Horse Regiment, Australian Imperial Force
Middle East 1914–1919

F arriers were in great demand by the Australian Light Horse, so when Harold Arthur Mertin joined up in 1914 he was welcomed with open arms.

He had learned his trade in the blacksmith shop at Eden Valley where he worked the forge, shoed the horses and fitted steel rims to wagon wheels.

The Australian Government had promised to provide four regiments of Light Horse to 'fight in the British cause', but by the end of the war 14 regiments were in action.

Harold Mertin sailed through the training period during which recruits had to prove their ability on horseback. Those who failed were transferred to other units.

About this time, Harold met a young lady, Jessie Kendrick, who was working in a photographer's shop in Adelaide. It was love at first sight but there was a war to be fought and Harold had signed up for the duration. He was soon on his way to the Middle East, but before he left he twice went Absent Without Leave to visit Jessie and suffered terms of detention as a result.

Apart from a photograph or two of his sweetheart, Harold had one other precious item to take with him on his travels—a camera. He soon became adept at its use and recorded many historic moments throughout his war experiences.

The 9th Light Horse Regiment, raised in Victoria and South Australia, together with the 10th from Western Australia and the 8th from Victoria, formed the 3rd Light Horse Brigade. They were sent to help defend Egypt from the Turks, along with the 1st and 2nd Light Horse Brigades and the New Zealand Mounted Rifles. Collectively, they became the Anzac Mounted Division.

Farrier Sergeant Harold Mertin at work.

While most of his regiment went to fight at Gallipoli, Harold was ordered to stay with the horses. After the regiment returned from Gallipoli in December 1915, he found himself caught up in fighting in defence of Egypt.

Over the next few years, he fought in many battles including Romani, El Arish, Gaza and Beersheba.

In his book *Farrier Sgt Mertin: The 9th Light Horse Regiment in the Middle East*, Harold's son, Ron, provides a history of the movements of the Regiment during World War I.

The first big battle was Romani.

In August 1916 a massive Turkish force was preparing for a second attack on the Suez Canal. Intelligence reports indicated that a strong body of Turks was to make an attempt on the Allied forces at the Canal and that they were assembled near Bir El Abd.

It was necessary for the British forces to head out into the Sinai desert to block the Turks from Romani—a crucial group of oases and cisterns in a great waste of sand dunes.

Orders were issued for the 3rd [Light Horse] Brigade to march out in one hour's time and be prepared to travel as light as possible. At the stated time the regiment was on

9th Light Horse Camp.

parade with a strength of 21 officers and 415 other ranks plus 459 horses. All wheeled transport was left behind.

The Turks, who had 20,000 men and heavy guns, attacked and tried to seize the railhead at Romani. Between 19 July and 12 August the brunt of the battle fell on the Australian Light Horse and the New Zealand Mounted Rifles.

The 3rd Light Horse [Brigade] were forced back by sheer numbers. Near Bir Nagid the enemy opened up heavy fire on A Squadron of the 9th Regiment, which was then joined by B Squadron and, between them, they were able to push forward. By the end of the day they had taken over 400 prisoners.

Conditions for the men and horses were harsh, to say the least. Water was extremely scarce.

They were under the tropical sun without shelter and the white glare of the sand seemed to scorch the skin and blind the eyes. The temperature was frequently over 120 degrees [49°C] in the shade, the men only had water bottles filled once daily. Horses could only be watered when suitable wells were found and at the most got a small drink every 24 hours.

By now, Brigadier-General J R Royston had taken over command of the 3rd Light Horse Brigade. Harold obviously admired the man and wrote: 'He is one of the best we have ever had or are likely to have and as game as you can get him. He could ride all day with the best of them and be just as good for a man of his age.'

In December 1916, the 3rd Light Horse Brigade took part in the general advance on El Arish, a large mud brick town close to the sea. The 9th Regiment camped in full view of the town for a day, extra rations were drawn and all surplus gear disposed of.

Then, at 6 pm, they joined up with other convoys and all were to be in position by daybreak.

The enemy opened fire with heavy and accurate shelling at ranges of 1000 yards [900 m] and 2000 yards [1800 m]. The ground around the town was quite flat and by 2 pm the line had advanced to within 500 yards [460 m]. When it reached 25 yards [20 m] there was a rush forward. Many of the Turks were bayoneted before surrendering.

The Air Service gave support and skimmed the enemy trenches dropping light bombs and the Lewis machine gun teams had their first taste of action. The regiment handed over nearly 160 enemy taken from the trenches. Next day they started on the long journey to Maghdaba where the prisoners were held, before returning to El Arish.

The enemy still held the fortified palace of Maghdaba with about 2000 men, 23 miles [37 km] up the Wadi Arish. At 8 pm on 22 December the forces assembled and marched on, reaching the enemy lines at dawn, taking up positions under the protection of sandhills.

The Light Horse, moving at a fast trot, came under heavy fire while riding across the front. The attack progressed well but slowly, with the ground favouring the enemy. At 3 pm the enemy was intensely bombarded. A rush was made at 4 pm and the Turkish resistance collapsed. There were 1200 prisoners taken and a large number of Turkish to be buried.

The young Australian Light Horsemen who now rode into Palestine along the desert battle paths of Napoleon and the Crusaders were very different figures from the eager young men who had flocked to the muddy training camps of winter Australia.

They were maturing and quickly developed their own style. As they moved around with the slouching gait of the Australian countryman at home, an observer described them as 'tired looking' but when ready for action, the observer noted, the same men could show 'an almost miraculous note of expectant eagerness'.

For the first time, the Australians entered enemy territory, passing across the border between Egypt and Palestine. The enemy had their main position at Rafa with an estimated 3000 men and a field of fire on all sides.

After a tough day of fighting, Rafa was taken with small losses to the Brigade and before 2000 Turkish reinforcements could arrive.

The next battle was for Gaza but this ended in withdrawal after the infantry was badly mauled by the Turks. Then new planes arrived, followed by the long-awaited tanks but, in the meantime, the Turks had increased their fortifications and boosted the number of troops along the Gaza-Beersheba line.

Once again the Turks defended stoutly and the Allies suffered heavy casualties, bringing about important changes in General Headquarters staff.

Minor operations then took place and continued from April to October 1917. The duties of the 9th Regiment in this period were to carry out regular reconnaissance, patrolling on horseback, in the Gaza area and around Atawinch.

During this period many skirmishes with the enemy took place. To shelter the men from the fierce heat, large square pits were dug and roofed with timber and grass matting, being large enough to accommodate eight men. The presence of large black scorpions and tarantula spiders proved a source of annoyance, but the men took advantage of this and waged scorpion and tarantula fights by placing one of each in a biscuit tin.

Troopers of the 9th Light Horse.

Finally, the decision was made to attack Beersheba and the 9th Regiment marched out over a very rough track. Two days later the signal for the attack to start was given. The 9th Regiment was heavily shelled but reached Tel-El-Saba, about 3 miles west of Beersheba, without casualties.

> Just before sunset, the 4th Brigade was seen to make a magnificent charge against the enemy trenches. Although mounted and armed with only a rifle and bayonet, they galloped clean over the enemy positions causing the utmost consternation amongst the Turks and this charge can be said to have decided the day.

The men of the 9th Regiment were then involved in a number of operations and even managed a short spell of rest and recreation, including time off to visit the town of Jaffa and its huge orange groves.

Once Amman had been captured the troops moved on to take Damascus.

> By 5 am the Regiment had crossed the river by the bridge at Dumar and the main road into the city was found to be almost completely blocked with dead or dying men, animals and disabled transport vehicles, the terrible execution of the previous day. The wounded were carried to the grassy banks to await our ambulances and the dead to await burial. The road was eventually cleared.

After more mopping up operations, the Regiment headed back through Damascus, Kuteife and Hom. During this journey word came through that the Turks had asked for and been granted an armistice and hostilities would cease on 31 October 1918. The Regiment continued on to Tripoli, in Lebanon, and camped in the olive groves on the edge of the city of Mwejdelaya.

On 11 November, the Germans were also granted an armistice. In the harbour, ships let off red, white and green flares and screeched their sirens until the boilers ran out of steam.

Now that the war was over, many of the Light Horsemen were disappointed to learn they would not be able to take their mounts home with them. Because of quarantine regulations it would have been impossible to take tens of thousands of horses back to Australia.

The horses were divided into four categories, A, B, C and D, with the first two transferred to the British 5th Yeomanry Brigade (Cavalry), and the other two groups due to be shot. The view was that they would not be well treated if sold to the locals and it would be more merciful to shoot them.

Just as it seemed the 9th Regiment would be departing for Australia, they were sent back to Egypt to help control the uprising known as the Egyptian Rebellion. The local Muslim population rioted against the British, tearing up railway lines, cutting telephone lines and attacking and killing British and other Europeans.

The 9th Regiment was detailed to proceed to Zig Zag and Tel-el-Kebir for the guarding of the railway line. The Regiment was also required to guard the aerodrome. When trouble was encountered, a few shots would soon put all ideas of resistance out of their minds. Many of the locals were arrested on charges of murder and pillage.

At last the 9th Regiment boarded the *Oxfordshire* and headed for home, stopping briefly at Colombo, and arriving at Fremantle on 4 August, exactly five years to the day of the declaration of war.

Horses at El Arish.

When Harold Mertin returned to his home in the Eden Valley of South Australia, he was one of only 38 of the original 400 men who left in February 1915 with the 9th Light Horse Regiment to have served until war's end.

He soon became engaged to Jessie Kendrick but nearly didn't make it to the altar. Once, when Jessie was visiting Eden Valley, the couple were out in a buggy when a double barrel shotgun resting between the seats discharged. After surviving all the fighting in the Middle East with nothing more than severe malaria and some shrapnel wounds to his hands, Harold Mertin received the full blast of the shotgun in his chest.

Jessie, a city girl, had the presence of mind to control the horse and make the return journey of 32 km to the hospital at Mount Pleasant. Harold lost two or three of his ribs but was made of stern stuff and recovered to marry Jessie a few months later.

Supplied by Ron Mertin of the ACT

'WEATHER BEAUTIFUL. HEALTH INDIFFERENT. PROSPECTS BRIGHT. SPIRITS HIGH'

Gunner Ronald Sinclair
114th Howitzer Battery, Australian Field Artillery
Australian Imperial Force
Egypt, France, Belgium 1915–1919

Ronald Sinclair lived for letters from home, and wrote plenty himself during his three and a half years away at war. In particular, he wrote regularly to his sweetheart, Adelene, telling her about his feelings, the war and his philosophy on all sorts of matters.

Occasionally the war got in the way of his letter writing, but even in the midst of battle he would still try to make time to write. He wrote at least 66 letters to Adelene during the war. On 20 May 1918, he was in a flippant mood.

> My Darling Old Ad, Here we go again. This time seated in a beautiful hole in the ground. Just room for two to lie down in & it's a case of when one turns we all turn. The job is to watch the wiley Hun & see he doesn't pinch any of the villages or some equally silly thing.
>
> Anyhow, we're here. Two of us & being here we make the most of the opportunity to drop a line or two to our own separate 'best little girl in all the world'. Only the other chap is unfortunate, he's married.
>
> However, the war has been, is, & will be carrying on much the same as a decent war should carry on. Not causing too much trouble & not interfering with the glorious weather which is gladdening the hearts of the people who want fine weather i.e the Huns.
>
> Personally I've been enjoying the war for the past fortnight or so. I've been a waggon line soldier & as such appropriated the jobs of 'cooks batman', linesman, telephone mechanic, Bookmaker and Poker Player.

Gunner Ronald Sinclair (front row, centre) and mates.

The first because it's better than grooming donkeys & the food is excellent as also the bed; the second two jobs I took on because they exempted me from all parades, the fourth I took on because I thought I could make some money at the sports & the last one I thought an enjoyable and profitable way of passing the evenings. The last one was the only one in which my judgement erred & by it I lost all I won at the sports, namely 200 francs, i.e about £8.

When the battery pulled in to its present position we found the adjacent village had been left in a hurry by the inhabitants & lots of good things were to be had for the asking. Consequently we lived high for a while.

Then when I went to the waggon lines I took up my residence with the cook in a caravan salvaged from the aforesaid village and there we lived like lords.

A couple of days ago one of the lads went ransacking the cupboards & Im sure youd have like to be there. You should see all the nice frilly things we found. Our shirts had done duty for quite a considerable time and wanted a spell. They got it. Now myself & the cooks may be seen arrayed not in issue shirts but in nice lace topped garments which certainly suit us down to the ground. If we wanted to we could also change our other garments but —. It's a beautiful caravan. Just a nice size for two. Big double bed. Stove wardrobe cupboard etc and some other bed furniture. I said a nice size for two. As a matter of fact its occupants at present number 5.

Along with the caravan we have added the following to the battery's list.

1 lamb blown up by a shell about three times but alive & doing well.
1 goat which has since changed to 1 goat and 1 kid, the dearest little kid in the world.
1 dog just like Bruce. He & I are great mates.

All we want now is a few nice young ladies to come and look after us & we'd think we were at home.

Now my fine young lady. What do you mean by inciting me to commit an offense prejudicial to good military order & discipline.

I never thought you were a girl like that Ad. I always had you in mind as a nice loving girl who would encourage a man to do gallant deeds etc. And now I find you are false. All my ideals are dashed to the ground. Here I am over here trusting you and what do you do. Again I ask what do you do. You deliberately say in your letter that when I go to Blighty again I ought to buy a camera. Now know ye that 'any Officer Non Commissioned officer or man having in his possession a camera will be tried by court martial and the penalty will be made as severe as possible.' So saith the orders.

So Im afraid Darling I cant oblige by getting one. I have often thought of running the risk & getting one so that from the observation post I could snap some of the beautiful barrages but the game is not worth the candle and Ive not done so.

Never mind Ad. Ill tell you all about the different things when I get home. Just fancy a shady nook up the Lane Cove, you & I & my diary & we'll fight the war all over again.

As I said before we had a sports day at the Waggon Lines the other day. And a Hun observation balloon looking right down on us. The squarehead must have been a sport though as he didn't interfere with us at all.

Three days ago I saw the best sight of the war. A Hun aeroplane was about 10,000 ft over our battery & one of our planes tackled him. The fight that followed was worth going miles to see. They both used up all their ammunition and then the flying began. Two more of our chaps came along but they wanted to get the machine intact so instead of firing at him they yarded him into a paddock & forced him to land. Of course we all flew over expecting to see some grizzled old fighter step out but imagine our surprise when out hopped a lad of 20 smoking a cigarette and his first words were 'It was ver goot'. He was as game as any man could be & the chap that brought him down landed & rushed up & shook hands with him. The machine was a triplane. If possible I will send home one of the souvenirs I took off the plane.

Well Darling the light is failing so I will have to put a finish to this note. Oh and by the way you are making me curious. In your last two letters you said you had been dreaming about me but wouldn't tell me what it was. Now last night I was dreaming about you and for spite I wont tell you what it was & it was so nice too.

Once again wishing you very many happy returns of my lucky day etc your birthday, I will conclude.

With fondest love, Ron

A week later his next letter was rather shorter and more to the point.

Just to carry on with the good work.
I am back at the guns again now & having a pretty good time, The violin we 'bought' in Corbie is getting some hurry up.
Anxiously waiting for some mail to come to hand.
Expecting the Hun to attack any time now but not the least bit alarmed.
Weather beautiful.
Health indifferent.
Prospects bright.
Spirits High.
Best love, Ron

Despite having survived all that the Germans had thrown at him, Ron found the news that Germany had surrendered to be something of an anticlimax. He had other things on his mind. He had written to Adelene a month earlier confessing to an indiscretion with a young lady while on leave in Scotland. He had told Ad that he had to be honest with her and asked for her forgiveness. He anxiously awaited her reply.

On 11 November 1918, he wrote to her again.

My Dearest old Girl,

In a deserted village, in a partly demolished house, beside a nice fire, and having just heard the glorious news that Germany had accepted an armistice under our own terms, and feeling as happy as possible under the circumstances, I am taking the opportunity of sending a chaser to my last letter.

I have wondered a lot how you accepted my last couple of notes and although I know what I want to tell you I can't bring myself to say it. I can quite understand what you will think of me but still Ad I think you must admit I had a big temptation to pal up with the first decent girl I met after being so long out of civilisation. What I want you to do if you will Ad is to consider what I have told you & if you think I have offended you past forgiveness, please say so.

I did not realise till I received your letter containing the snaps yesterday what I had done. [Ad's letter was obviously written and sent before she received Ron's confession.]

Thanks very much for the snaps old girl, they were great. I studied them for an hour and could quite easily imagine I was back home. Then memory began to get busy and as I had just received the first letter from home since poor old Dad died I can tell you I went to bed pretty miserable. It seems hard to think that after living so long he should die just when things began to look best. Still I suppose it is for the best & we must accept the inevitable with good grace.

Thanks very much Ad for your sympathy. I know how you feel about it old girl.

But let us get to the good news. Isn't it simply great. 3 years and 9 days since I left Australia & now at last the end is in sight. And I can tell you Ad we've seen some fighting since June last & I can scarcely credit it that I have been able to live through it all without a scratch. Someones prayers must have been heard.

The next thing now is the peace terms & then home. Can you realise what home means to us over here. Back to your own people & those we love, and once back I cant see them shifting me out of Australia again. Ive seen all the war I want to thank you & Ive seen all the world I want to and theres no place like Australia.

It's not known if Ad replied to Ron or if she met him when his boat docked. But they married eventually in June 1920 and had seven children.

Life wasn't easy for them. Not only did they have a large family to provide for, Ron found it difficult to cope. The accumulated effects of all the trauma he had suffered—the loss of both his parents, the years of separation and deprivation, the witnessing of violence and death and living with the constant threat to his own life throughout the war—took a heavy toll.

Ad died suddenly following a heart attack at the age of 56. Her loss was a great blow to Ron but he lived another 16 years before dying of cancer at the age of 74.

Ron's letters have been collated by his daughter, Monica, and reproduced in a book *Dear Ad . . . Love Ron: A Personal Story of Love and War Told in the Letters of a Young WWI Soldier.*

Supplied by Monica Sinclair of New South Wales

Lance-Corporal W L Hatcher
22nd Battalion, Australian Imperial Force
The Somme, France 1916

Casualty Clearing Stations (CCS) were the first stop for many soldiers wounded in World War I. These advanced surgical stations were located as close to the action as possible.

They were so close to the fighting that the Germans often shelled them, and the nurses of the Australian Army Nursing Service (AANS) felt they were as good as in the front line. Their work involved long hours, particularly during major battles, when hundreds of casualties would be brought in for emergency surgery to be followed by evacuation to rear hospitals.

Many soldiers were so badly wounded when brought to a CCS that little could be done to help, apart from giving comfort, a kind word and a smile. The simple action of removing the soldiers' boots, which often hadn't been off their feet for many days, was enough to bring cries of appreciation.

Despite the long hours spent nursing the wounded, the nurses also undertook tasks which had nothing to do with medical treatment. They would sit and listen to soldiers as they talked longingly of loved ones back home and, in many instances, agreed to write letters for those unable to do so.

Often it was their sad task to write to families to tell them of their son's last hours before he died, passing on messages which were mostly to send love and to tell the families not to worry.

Sister M Aitken was working at the 3rd CCS at Puchevillers, about 19 km northeast of Amiens in France in August 1916 when Lance-Corporal William Leonard Hatcher of the 22nd Battalion AIF was brought in.

Lance-Corporal William Hatcher in uniform.

The 20-year-old soldier from Goyura in Victoria was severely wounded during fighting on the Somme and died the following day on Monday, 7 August 1916.

Sister Aitken wrote to his parents, Thomas and Eliza Hatcher, at his request, made just before he died.

> I regret I have the worst possible news for you. He was admitted into hospital here on the 6th, severely wounded in the abdomen and although everything possible was done to save him he gradually got much worse and passed peacefully away this morning at 10.30.
>
> Shortly before his death I asked for your address. He was delighted when I said I would write you. 'My only message to home is tell Mother I am wounded, give her my fondest love and ask her not to worry.'
>
> He was such a sweet nice patient and we can understand, just a little, what his loss means to you. No words of mine can comfort you in any way but please accept my sincerest sympathy & admiration for your brave young boy.
>
> My heart ached for you so far away from your loved one. Rest assured we did what we could for him. He had a nice comfortable bed & every attention from us all. We did our best but the issue was in God's hands.
>
> I regret very much to write you such sad tiding but no word of any kind would be worse for you to bear. Your boys end was peace & the look on his face afterwards was sufficient evidence to make one realise his life had been well spent—he seemed so contented & happy.

Sister Aitken went on to say Lance-Corporal Hatcher would have a military funeral and that he would be buried in Puchevillers Cemetery nearby.

> It's reserved for officers and men of the British Army. Our men look after it & everything is so neat. There are flowers on each grave.

And having written to Mr and Mrs Hatcher, Sister Aitken went back to work tending the wounded.

Supplied by K J Hatcher of Victoria

'Please accept my sincerest sympathy & admiration for your brave young boy.'

Wounded Australian soldiers in France, 1916.

TOGETHER AGAIN BEFORE THE NEXT XMAS'

Sergeant Syd Green
Australian Army Services Corps, Australian Imperial Force
France 1916–1917

 rs Mary Green was busy at home on 9 January 1917 when she heard a knock on her front door. Like hundreds of mothers before and after her, her heart missed a beat when she found the local parish priest on the step.

He had been given the thankless task of informing her that her son, Sergeant Syd Green of 3rd Depot Unit of Supply, Australian Army Service Corps, had died of gunshot wounds at the 2/2nd London Casualty Clearing Station on 28 December 1916.

It was inevitable with the large number of casualties in World War I that many a parent received a letter from their son fighting in Europe after being told of his death. And so it was with Mary Green.

Syd had been away for two years but he and his mother had corresponded regularly. She had sent him a parcel of 'goodies' for Christmas and he and his mates had made short work of it on the train journey to their latest camp.

On Christmas Day, Sergeant Green worked issuing supplies to the troops but managed a few quiet moments to write to his mother, thanking her for the parcel. It was to be the last letter he ever wrote.

> My dearest Mother, today is Xmas Day and the second I have spent away from home, and I hope the last. I have just arrived back at camp, the rest of our chaps are working late so I have the tent to myself and have a few minutes to write.
>
> We worked as usual today issuing supplies, and there was the same amount of rain, mud and slush so there wasn't much to remind us of Xmas. A few miles away our guns are pounding away at the Germans and sometimes the sky is lit up by the flashes. Star shells rise and fall like brilliant sky rockets and everything is just War.

Sergeant Syd Green with mate .

Syd was obviously looking forward to what must have seemed like a sumptuous feast and found time to tell his mother who had helped provide the food.

> Tonight about 9.30 pm we will have our Xmas dinner of roast beef and potatoes, roast turkey (kindly given to us by the officer in charge of our column) and plum duff (issued by the Army but subscribed for by the people of England) so we should have a good time and enjoy ourselves.

> I hope you got my letter from Rouen saying I received your Xmas parcel, everything was great, Mother, and we disposed of the eatables in the train on our journey here, but I'm afraid I was too excited to thank you for it. However, you know how grateful I am for all you do for me and I can only hope to repay it all when I get home.

Syd sought to comfort his mother, who was obviously worried about her other son, Bert, going away to fight against the Germans. Whether he truly thought the end of war was in sight or not, he certainly gave that impression.

> I had another lovely letter from you a few days ago but am sorry you're missing Bert and so sad about him coming away. Mother, he'll be as right as a bank and will probably arrive here in time to see the finish of it all and take me home.

> You take it from me, 1917 is the last lap of the war and Fritz will throw in the sponge at the first opportunity and he'll get the shock of his life very soon. Now don't you worry about Bert he can look after himself and ditto me, so we'll all be together again before the next Xmas.

> Well Mother, I'll have to say goodbye again with love to everybody I know and hoping you are keeping well and in good spirits. Best love and kisses from your loving son, Syd.

Sergeant Syd Green died of multiple gunshot wounds three days after he wrote this letter.

A memorandum dated 9 January 1917 from Major E D'Arcy of the 1st Military District, Australian Military Forces, in Brisbane, addressed to the Senior Chaplain, Roman Catholic Denomination, asks him to 'please break the news to Mrs Mary Elizabeth Green and convey the deep sympathy of King, Queen and Commonwealth Government in the loss she and the army have sustained.'

While Sergeant Green died, aged 21, just days after eating his Christmas dinner in 1916, he had enjoyed a much more organised event the previous year while on T S *Suffolk*.

In true wartime humour, the ship staged its Xmas Day dinner with a tongue-in-cheek menu.

FEDERAL STEAM NAVIGATION COY. LTD
TRANSPORT A 23
T. S. SUFFOLK

TROOPS MENU
DINNER XMAS DAY 1915

Shallots au Natural

Consomme a la Rubbish

Potage Skilli

Whitebait Nextrip

Saute de la Suffolk Lingo
Curried Rabbit Alf-onso
Underdun Roast Surloin of Beef minus Yorko
Roast Head of Pork Quick Style
Stuffed Mutton not Dinkum
Roast Turkey a la Perhaps

Baked and Boiled Potatoes Fermento
Peas aux Cardcounters

Plum Pudding Hard and Sauce (tasteless)
Trifle Mortrouble

Cheese (nippy)   Dessert (byenbie)

Pumpkin, Marrow, and other Fruits in Season

Weak Tea   Coffee Grounds

Sarto 4d extra

WINE LIST   P.T.O.

Supplied by Marjorie Whimp of Queensland

'LIKE PUTTING UP CARDBOARD NINE-PINS IN A HURRICANE'

Sergeant Clair Whiteside
59th Battalion, Australian Imperial Force
France 1916–1918

Thomas Clair Whiteside was a prolific letter writer. Throughout his service in World War I, he wrote regularly to his parents and sister, sending over 200 letters in the three years he was abroad.

Clair Whiteside enlisted on 17 July 1915. After initial training at Seymour about 100 km north of Melbourne, he set sail on *Ulysses* for the Middle East. Over the next few months he underwent further training until he was finally sent to France late in June 1916.

It wasn't long before he was thrown headlong into one of the fiercest battles of the war at Fromelles in which the 5th Division AIF suffered 5533 casualties in just one night. Clair Whiteside was wounded in the first attack and described what happened in a letter home, written from the 3rd Southern General Hospital in Oxford, England, on 28 July 1916.

> Dear Mother, on the morning of the 19th plans were given out to the NCOs who in turn had to get their sections and grenade parties up to the pitch. After dinner, a pot of old pig potatoes and a lump of PIG, we went down to the trenches to our relative positions. Did not get there without some trouble for communication trenches were under heavy high explosive fire. Our platoon sergeant, Wally White, was killed and a private got buried. Never learnt who he was, though I gave an order for the last man to clear him out.
>
> Well, we hugged the trenches for a few hours while the curtain raiser, the artillery duel was on. When its chief job was done, viz wire-cutting, the hour was up. The first thin line of heroes get on the parapet and make off for the opposing lines. The first lines fare the best—for the terrible machine-gun is deadly once he sees the game is properly on. It looked like putting up cardboard nine-pins in a hurricane—only it was

---

Sergeant Thomas Clair Whiteside.

human beings who were facing up to it. A good number were wounded before the charge, but a short distance into No-Man's Land and the grass was thick with them.

I was holding my rifle over my knee, in a sitting position against the parapet, when an ugly lump of shrapnel hit the rifle near where I was holding it. It cut through the wood-work and made a good dint in the barrel. Number one lucky one. But I had plenty more let-offs awaiting me. Advanced in short rushes taking advantage of any cover. No-Man's Land had a lagoon and ditches—waist deep in water. Waded through the ditches glad of the cooling off but the lagoon had to be got around. It was at the ends of the lagoon where planks crossed a ditch that the machine-guns got their haul. It was jump jump jump over some poor beggar the whole time, but it was pat yourself on the back at the other side.

The going on the other side was better and with the chaps well spread out, and taking plenty of advantage of the grass, we were not suffering so heavily. Of course plenty were unlucky and came in full contact with one of Fritz's iron foundries. I never knew I would be so anxious to get at Fritz as I was. I simply couldn't put any time on the grass. Called to a few chaps beside me and cleared on a bit further, until in a very short while, I was ahead of the first two lines. The order for the 3rd wave was not to stop at the enemy's first line but to carry on to his supports. But here I got pulled up. I arrived at Fritz's front door and was quizzing around to see if our fellows had knocked anywhere. A machine-gun was rat ta tat tat tapping in the grass a few yards to my left and it was while trying to learn something about its crew that a sniper caught me. Got a nasty one on the head and of course, for a minute, thought I was done for. Had the sensation a poor old rabbit gets when you hit him on the ears. Did not go round in a circle like poor old raw bunny but I can tell you it seemed to lift me bodily. However I had a heaven-sent vision of beef tea and chicken and thinking Fritz might not have too many chooks on hand, or not feeling disposed to give them out to the fighting 'kangaroos', I made towards our own base and the ticklish part of the game had just started.

Could not crawl straight back over heights and hollows. That would have made an avenue in the grass which would have invited a machine-gun to turn down. Any undue movement of the grass, and if you didn't know before, you soon found out what real war was all about. I absolutely astonished myself on my scouting capacity. Zigzagged twenty or thirty yards back to my left then crawled forward into a thick patch and zigzagged back to the right. The first 30 yards two bullets went through my old iron helmet and I just recorded a hit on the right shoulder—now only a scratch mark.

Came on my chum, Cpl. Frank Dixon a short way back. He, with four or five others, was taking the wisest course under the circumstances, waiting for something to turn up. Don't know how they fared. I kept the cover of my old gas helmet jammed up to my forehead to stop the bleeding. At this stage our own artillery, thinking they had not opened up the way enough, started again. A shell lobbed in the exact spot where I had been hit and once more I counted my blessings and decided for a still safer spot. There was a dry ditch three or four feet [about 1 m] deep on a rise on the enemy side of the lagoon. Worked back to it and found it full but it was stacks on the mill in a position like that. It was 'mind my arm—get off my legs'. The whole principle was to keep down and hug terra firma. Here I stuck till after dark and it was a warm spot. Was in the direct line of fire between the well-shelled tracks to the side of the lagoon and German guns working from straight ahead and almost every angle.

It's interesting, though none too pleasant, speculating whether you are going to get the full effects of a shell, a mild earthquake or merely a ton or two of dirt on top of you. Had my old helmet lying on my head. I could not sum up enough energy of the kind to put my field dressing on. Did not feel shellproof but did feel totally indifferent as to how much dirt lobbed on me. The old ditch shook many a time suggesting there was a way through to Australia. Wouldn't have taken it if it had opened up—I don't think! After the programme of shells and flare-rockets had continued for a couple of hours into the night, one of our company fellows, Bill Skinner from Trafalgar and I decided to make a bolt for our trenches. There seemed little likelihood of the curtain ringing down for the night and no probability of refreshments. It's a most unpleasant side of warfare, lying out in a battlefield—wounded, maybe perfectly helpless with no chance of aid being given you. It must be bitterly cruel to the man nearly out to it.

Well, Skinner and I crawled and hustled like old nick when no flare-shells were about, avoiding the worst shelled spots—lay in shell-holes and long grass when the flares were up. Had a machine-gun turned on us two or three times. Waded waist-deep in water for a few yards down one trench. Had a little difficulty getting through some of our own barbed wire but finally bawled out 59th and dropped down in a trench full of friends. They took us to their dressing station where we both had rough field dressings put on.

As the communication trenches were being blown to pieces they advised us to abide where we were for the night. That I did and slept the remainder of the night with my head in the old tin helmet. Better than I have slept since.

Next morning I followed a number of stretcher cases down to the main dressing station. From there had a motor ambulance trip to Sailly, to the 14th Brigade Field Hospital. Everyone was inoculated there—slept the night. We were put into different classes and in the morning sent off by train to different places, many like myself to Boulogne where we arrived at night. Had an ambulance trip of a few miles over cobbled streets and finally camped in a small hospital near shipping accommodation.

The next day a fair percentage of us embarked on a beautifully fitted little hospital boat [HS *Dieppe*] for 'Blighty'. Arrived at Dover in a short time, was put on a hospital train and was soon in the very good quarters I'm now in. Slept better the last two nights. Can give you but little account as to how my companions have fared. The greater number are undergoing repairs. Don't know how many are underground. Have not heard how Will O'Sullivan or Alan Russell fared. Vic Stafford got to the dressing station on a stretcher the same time as I wobbled in. Cpl Stan Barr and Sgt Ball were in the same hospital train to Boulogne as was Capt Hewitt and a few other officers. The last I heard about 16 Platoon, there were only two left unwounded.

I'm away from the censor now so I can tell you a few little things about the front. There were many ugly sights at the first dressing station. But there were many who had hours of lying out before they would ever see a dressing.

Will never forget the few hours, which seemed as many days, lying low till dark and then crawling when night arrived, when no flares were up. Listened with interest and speculation as to where the next shell was going to lob. Here she comes and you hug old terra firma. An almighty bang—the earth trembles. Keep your head well covered with the iron helmet and wait for the pieces. Smile with relief if it's only a two-pound clod of earth that gets you full in the back, then have a look at the smoke and count your blessings in yards. I think to myself: 'Don't be too inquisitive—machine-guns are more searching than shells'. We were in fighting order with haversacks on our backs—tin dixies placed as when in marching order. I was evidently spotted, though I was in a shallow gutter, and a machine-gun put bullet-holes through the tin. I later carried on to a shell-hole.

Often wonder what happened to many a chap I passed lying helpless in the grass. For my part I was strong and had all my wits about me and it was only through acting on every inspiration that, with God's help, I got out of it.

Clair Whiteside lost some personal belongings on the field. Four months later, on 15 November 1916, an unknown person sent three photographs to the *Sydney Mail* for identification. They were recognised by relatives who had them sent on to his mother, Sally.

Once he recovered from his wounds, he was eventually sent back to the fighting in France but was wounded a second time at Bullecourt in April 1917. This time he was hit by shrapnel from an Allied shell. He was later sent to England for an operation on his nose, unconnected to the wound he had received.

During his recovery period, Clair Whiteside was able to get out and about a bit and witnessed a small riot involving Australian troops.

Though it took place a few weeks ago I do not remember telling you of the burning down of the Blood House—that classical and privately-run entertainment near the camp. Well, it was crowded one night, as usual, with an impatient crowd of 'kangars' waiting for something to chuck off at. Something went wrong with the cinematograph gear (the better half of the show consisted of pictures). The boys demanded their money back. The manager did not agree to paying out, so the men promptly piled up the wooden forms and set them and the whole caboose alight, hauled the piano out; got the regimental buglers to play the *Last Post* on the place while some not particularly gifted accompanist played *Keep the home fires burning*.

As the fire threatened to subside the piano was chucked in to help things along and complete the job. The manager tried to combat popular opinion with a fire hose but it was very soon cut in a dozen pieces. Colonel Knox appeared on the closing scene but did not appear to be very moved by the spectacle. As Commandant of the Depot his appearance was hardly welcome, but the boys have all summed him up as one of the best in the AIF.

A pretty big claim for damages was put in, including £50 for the piano and so much for bumper houses missed, but we have never heard what the winding up cost [was]. The Blood House is now a thing of the past and the neighbouring show, The Pavilion, has learned a lesson and is considerably improved, but for many nights afterwards the manager had the wind up. It was very funny the night of the burning, some of the village people were very excited and enquired of many of the more sober element amongst the boys—if they thought they would burn the whole town down. I heard one chap say; 'Nearly sure to mum', and the enquirer hastened off to gather her treasures. Some boys, these Anzacs. At times an unreasoning crowd.

While he showed some admiration for the actions at the Blood House, he was less than impressed by a group of Australians who had gone Absent Without Leave (AWL).

Numbers of our least brilliant specimens are AWL and camped in the various woods about. They come down into the camp after parade hours and gather in the necessary bawbees by gambling stunts of all kinds, cadging, and so on. Our Batt Major bailed up a piquet on the road into Warminster last Monday. He did not exactly congratulate them on their general appearance and execution of duty. He asked what battalion they were detailed from and when told his own he took their names by their pay books. When he got back he started to roar things up but soon found out that every man of them was absent without leave, and one had been for 18 months. So the next morning [4 June] a search of the surrounding country was organised to gather up all on duty or otherwise, with the result that the clink had about 50 extra patients waiting on a variety of charges. Some were sent off to France with the next draft, others have gone elsewhere, but the cells are still well filled and the call of the 'birds' for fags is loud and long but goes pretty much unheeded. Cigs are becoming too dear and bludging altogether too prevalent.

This morning, the old rig-me-rol of company parade—battalion parade with its various 'shuns' and then the march to the training ground. The band is nothing like as good as the depot band, still it acts like a whip to a run-down cab horse and even makes one feel fresh to the game, in spite of advancing age. Bayonet fighting, jerks and guard drill was the morning's programme. There are a few Tommy instructors amongst the staff and they provide some sport with their 'Chum and Woodbine' touches. Some of them are really smart, but if lacking in a sense of humour they do not get too much work out of the 'dinkums'.

The more one sees of both crowds the more one appreciates the independent fighting spirit of the Aussie. If it hasn't come out now years will show that he has been the best soldier maybe of the war. Whatever his individual position he considers himself the equal to anyone, whether the present finds him in the clink, batman to the Colonel, pushing a pen with his hair brushed back or cooking in close proximity to the beer canteen. He owns as much to rights and privileges as he can fathom and wherever he goes he has the air of owning the place. He is a wonder no doubt, but a chap is proud to be one of them.

Once more back in France, Clair Whiteside was involved in the Harbonnieres campaign in August 1918.

Had a lively, but great time of it since writing a week ago. A number of old pals are gone and others wounded but this time there was none of that feeling of the loss being all for nothing. The day was ours and Fritz was properly put to flight. There was no mistaking the fact that he was getting a beating at his own game—even in the way of organization—while individually, as usual, he couldn't stand on the same ground as the Aussie. Personally I saw a good deal of the novel side of the affair.

A special brigade section went over in tanks and from a novelty point of view I was glad to be in it, though in other respects it pays better to be with the battalion. Had a couple of days solid marching getting up near the front line with the tanks, and then to get right up to it on the night was a ticklish and slow job. Some little time before zero Fritz pelted us with a few gas shells. The tanks were lined up in a bit of a hollow when the bombardment started. Can only say it was some bombardment. Until being in one you could not have the faintest idea of what they are like. Regardless of what Fritz was likely to send over, we climbed the hill to see the effect on his lines and also to get a better view of the flashes of our guns, miles back. With the deafening row the whole effect is thrilling.

We were to take the final objective for the day so did not start for some time after the others had gone over. As we were going over Fritz's battered front line, prisoners from further on had been rounded up and were marching back in groups, up to one hundred strong, with a guard or two. Others were straggling back in ones, twos or threes, making for the safety of our back areas, 'toot sweet' and with their hands up, to show their perfect willingness to go unmolested. Further on they were made to do a good deal of the stretcher bearing. Their marching in fours was good. The most of them seemed to be not altogether displeased with the situation. Most, at any rate, were enjoying the fact that they were escaping with whole skins. Some of the wounded were pitiful sights, with their appeals for mercy.

The country for some distance was very flat, much of it in crop, about ripe, but badly blackened. Tracks of the smaller tanks could he seen all through it, where they had been skirmishing about for pockets of the enemy or for strong points. The advance was so rapid we did not get into our tanks for a few miles of the advance. Could only see the fighting in the distance. The scene soon changed into typical French country—villages on every side and as we neared the hand to hand go, if such you could call it (for a few Fritz took the risk of firing to the last before putting up their hands) his balloons spotted us. His artillery, especially when the tanks were finding any difficulty getting over obstacles, gave us some 'hurry up' with his shells. Then when we got right into it, a few of them were hit at point blank range.

It was terribly hot inside the tanks. Ours was overcrowded. I and another chap stuck on the back of it until nearly up to the objective. When Fritz started peppering us with machine-gun fire we went diplomatically to one side or the other. Ours was also the job to hold the line for the night. In the morning [29 August] a battalion went over the top of us and for a while got a very rough time of it, especially with machine-gun fire.

We went out carrying in wounded and soon after, when the atmosphere got a little healthier, many were out in their usual Aussie fashion, ratting the dead, friend and foe alike, a job which even now does not much appeal to me. One of our officers had his right arm blown off, badly wounded in the left arm and leg. Getting him into the trench was a short job, bandaged him up and got him to the dressing station. Wondering now if he pulled through. Didn't know him formerly as he is 6th Battalion man. A very decent little chap. I am afraid that he will have a hard time of it.

Clair Whiteside was involved in further heavy fighting around Peronne before the war came to an end three months later. He was one of the lucky ones given a quick passage home and he arrived in Melbourne on 15 January 1919.

Supplied by Elizabeth Whiteside of Victoria who has published the letters in a book A Valley in France

ABORIGINAL BOY SURVIVES FAMILY MASSACRE BUT DIES IN WAR

Private William Joseph Punch
1st Battalion, Australian Imperial Force
France 1917

A n Aboriginal boy who was the sole survivor of a brutal attack in which his entire family was massacred in 1880, was brought up by a white family in country New South Wales and later fought for Australia in World War I.

William Joseph Punch was wounded twice while fighting, first in Belgium and later in France. He was evacuated to England for treatment each time, but eventually died of pneumonia at Mont Dore Hospital in Bournemouth.

William Punch was a respected worker, a top sportsman and an accomplished musician before answering the call to sign up in 1915.

In January 1931, *Reveille* published a list of Aboriginal people from New South Wales who had served in the AIF. It listed 18 who had been killed or died in the war, 31 who had been wounded or gassed, and 56 others who had taken part. The paper said the list 'no doubt contained some omissions but at least emphasised how the Aborigines of New South Wales had rallied to the colours during the Great War.' According to articles written by Albert Speer MBE in the Goulburn and District Historical Society's newsletter in October 1992 and April 1993, the list failed to mention William Punch.

In his articles, Mr Speer said the man attributed with bringing William Punch to the area was John Siggs, the eighth child of Richard Siggs and Mary Sullivan. John had grown up at Pejar, where his father and mother had several small land holdings and also ran the old Pejar Inn.

John Siggs rode as a young man to the cattle on agistment from the Pejar, Woodhouselee and Roslyn areas to land surrounding Lake Cowal where the Regans, relatives to the Siggs, had landed interests.

Soldiers from the Goulbourn district of New South Wales before entrainment to Sydney on 27 February 1916. Private William Punch is in the centre of the middle row.

Speer wrote that it was commonly circulated that the Siggs family from North Queensland had brought back William Punch, but this was discounted by a story told to him by a lady in her nineties.

She had told him that Siggs, with other people from Roslyn and Woodhouselee, had taken cattle to the Bland. On their arrival at the Bland River one of the beasts was speared by some Aboriginal people and roasted and eaten. A retributory raid was conducted in the late night.

Young Siggs slept through it all, and the next morning he rode over to see the result and discovered among the dead bodies a small baby who was trying to suckle from his dead mother's breast. He uttered the words, 'Oh, this is bloody murder, I will have no part of this', according to the old lady, and picked up the baby and rode home to Pejar.

'So William Joseph Punch's early life commenced with a supportive and loving family group,' Speer wrote. 'The reason for the Queensland origins story was, I am sure, to cover up the lad's birthplace so he would not wish to seek out his relatives, as presumably these no longer existed.'

Speer wrote that a Mrs Mary Fingleton had revealed that the nephews and nieces of John Siggs were taught by a governess at the old Pejar House and William Punch rode with the Siggs family to music lessons in Crookwell. He was a noted musician and a well-educated man. He was also a great sportsman and had taken part in local sports committees.

Speer wrote that articles in the *Goulburn Evening Penny Post* on Woodhouselee up until 1915 recounted stories of William Punch's involvement in local activities—sports and musical entertainment and participation in the formation of the Woodhouselee Rifle Club.

'The advent of hostilities on the other side of the world featured largely in the press of the day and constant calls had been made for more recruits,' Speer wrote. 'W J Punch had answered that call and so on 31 December 1915 he enlisted in the Army. He gave as his next of kin a young member of the Siggs family, Oswald Gallagher. His service number was 5435. He was in camp at Goulburn Showground. He was one of the 300 soldiers honoured at an early Mass and breakfast on 27 February 1916 prior to entraining for Sydney.'

Speer wrote that William Punch was referred to as the mascot of the unit and was very popular with the troops. He and other soldiers apparently fell ill with mumps and were left behind in Egypt, but later joined the 1st Battalion.

William Punch saw action in Belgium and was wounded on 7 September 1916. He had written to the Siggs-Gallagher family on 3 September 1916 to say that he had been in England for nine days and was going to France. He mentioned gas drill, that he had made friends with a 'Bosker bloke' from Clear Hills, Roslyn, NSW, and that soon they would be in the front line in Belgium.

He was wounded again in France on 5 April 1917 and was sent back to England where he was nursed in Mont Dore Hospital, Bournemouth. He died of pneumonia on 29 August 1917. He is buried in the Bournemouth East Cemetery, Boscombe, in Plot X, Grave No. 185. He was recorded as having been aged 37 and a native of Queensland. Sister O'Shea, an Australian nurse serving at the hospital, wrote to the *Reveille* on 31 August 1931 about William Punch and supplied a photo of him in his hospital bed.

So, the story of William Joseph Punch, which began, reportedly, with gunfire in a creek-bed, ended tragically with gunfire in 1917 in the Great War.

Supplied by Geoff Speer of New South Wales

'THE KELLY GANG' RIDES AGAIN

Corporal Pat Reed
'The Kelly Gang'
6th Division Cavalry, Australian Imperial Force
Syria 1941

The Kelly Gang was one of the most unusual Allied fighting units during World War II. It was made up from an assortment of 70 or so men, mainly from C and B Squadron, 6th Division Cavalry, who rode captured horses in the Syrian campaign.

They were fighting against Vichy French troops who, under the command of General Henri Dentz, had sided with the Axis forces. The Vichy French were well armed and trained, many being from the French Foreign Legion, and were backed by Senegalese troops.

The British regarded it as essential to control Syria. If the Germans overran the country, they could threaten access to the Suez Canal and Cairo and also vital oil supplies for the Allies.

The 6th Division Cavalry had lost many of its tanks in earlier fighting against the Vichy French, who had mounted a far greater resistance than expected. The French had an excellent knowledge of the terrain, gained from years of operating in the region.

'The Kelly Gang' was formed to give much needed mobility over the rough terrain, much of which was unsuitable for tanks, and to provide protection on the flanks. It was the only Australian horsed cavalry unit to operate in action during the war.

The men were all experienced bushmen or former militia cavalry. Initially they were under the command of Lieutenant J F P Burt, who had shortly before taken over as CO of C Squadron, and, later, of Lieutenant A B Millard, who had been second-in-command of C Squadron.

Members of 'the Kelly Gang'. From left to right: Luke Monaghan, Ken McDonald, Cliff Brown, Monty Bennett, Alf Bruce and Pat Reed.

Although the unit operated for only a short time, about four weeks in June and July 1941, it carried out invaluable work. It covered the area from Bmeriq to Kafr Hamame over country so rough that, in some cases, patrolling was carried out on foot while the horses were left in the care of horse handlers.

Thirty-two horses that had been used by the French cavalry were captured during fighting at Rachaya el Fokhar. On 22 June, Brigadier F H Berryman, who was then in command of the 7th Division's artillery, ordered that a troop be formed from the ranks of the cavalry to act as a roving reconnaissance screen in the hills. He wanted protection for his eastern flank and it wasn't hard to find experienced riders from among the Australian ranks.

After an arduous, night-long ride to Bmeriq, the troops found the French saddles to be extremely uncomfortable and it became clear that more men and horses would be needed to enable two separate patrols to alternate in the difficult and tiring conditions. More captured horses were collected, new saddles were obtained and more bushmen were recruited for the unit.

'The Kelly Gang' carried rifles and Bren guns and roamed through the hills with pack horses carrying extra supplies. They gathered information and engaged the enemy, carrying out a number of raids and ambushes on Vichy French troops hidden in the mountain villages. They provided vital information on the location of enemy troops and artillery, kept incursions by enemy patrols to a minimum and, at the same time, protected the Allies' flanks.

The 'Gang' came under heavy fire on at least three occasions and were surprised to find that the French horses were not the least scared of the shelling directed at them, having been well trained by their previous owners.

Pat Reed was the cook for the 'Kelly Gang', so he was not involved in the raids. That didn't mean he was out of danger, however.

> Once, in the truck which I shared with the fettler, we were the last to leave the camp site. The mounted troops had left earlier. One wrong turn took us towards the enemy. Having corrected that mistake we headed downhill.
>
> On meeting a group of English engineers, we were told the Vichy French had been landing shells behind us all the way down. We hadn't heard a thing.
>
> When we reached our next camp site, which was in a terraced valley, the enemy decided to shell us again. The shells landed amongst the horses and mules lines but there were no injuries. Again the animals showed no sign of fright.

After that was over, we had prepared dinner for the boys when a voice was heard from the top of an 80-foot [24 m] cliff which we were against. There was an Arab with an unexploded shell in his arms, waiting to drop it down on us. We discouraged him.

'The Kelly Gang' was relieved on 3 July by members of B Squadron of the North Somerset Yeomanry and moved to the coastal region. Its members eventually returned to a more conventional role in armoured vehicles.

Supplied by Pat Reed of South Australia

'JEESE, I THOUGHT YOU WAS THE COOK!'

Commander Harrie 'Bug' Oliver
HMAS *Napier,* Royal Australian Navy
Mediterranean 1941

The Australian destroyer HMAS *Napier* was one of several ships that played a major role in the evacuation of Allied troops from Crete in May 1941, but she almost didn't make it.

Napier was steaming at full speed for Alexandria in the company of her sister ship HMAS *Nizam.* Both ships carried in excess of 700 troops, plucked from the shore at Sfakia during the night.

As soon as dawn broke, the ships were attacked by the *Luftwaffe* and put up a wall of fire. The rescued troops fired rifles and Bren guns in support of the ships' guns. Miraculously, both ships survived the attacks and the enemy aircraft eventually returned to base.

Then came an attack from a lone Ju 88 bomber. Captain Steve Arliss watched through his binoculars, judging where the bombs would fall and making a last minute alteration to the ship's course. The bombs narrowly missed but exploded beside the ship.

Napier came to a halt as her engines lost power and *Nizam* circled to see if she could help, all the while watching the skies anxiously for the return of enemy aircraft. In fact, the turbine feet were damaged, putting the engine out of action, and the oil fuel pump in the after boiler room was also broken.

Commander Harrie 'Bug' Oliver was the Engineer Officer on *Napier.* It was his job to keep the ship going. According to an account written by Rear-Admiral O H Becher, Oliver 'appeared on the bridge—quite unperturbed as usual. "Give me half an hour and we will be going again," he said to the Captain and sure enough, in that time, we were on our way at 16 knots.'

Commander Harrie 'Bug' Oliver in uniform.

We had no more nastiness from the Huns and entered Alexandria Harbour at about 7 pm to receive a rousing reception from the Fleet. We could not go astern so we were put alongside by tugs. Sir Andrew Cunningham slipped over the guard rails to give the Captain a big pat on the back. 'Bug' Oliver received a Mention in Despatches for his leadership in the engine room and outstanding ability in getting us going again so quickly. This was, I believe, one of the most worthy of the war and I believe should have been at least a DSC [Distinguished Service Cross].

'Bug' Oliver's own account described what happened to *Napier* after she returned to Alexandria.

After our second run to Sfakia, *Napier* spent several weeks moored in Port Said while a team of Suez Canal Co men removed two plates from our main deck, lifted our port high pressure turbine, and took it by lighter across to their work shops at Port Fuad.

The near miss which fractured our main and auxiliary machinery bases also bent that turbine shaft, making it unusable at full power. So the Port Fuad shop spun it in a lathe and skimmed the fore end shaft down a few thousandths to restore alignment, then re-metalled the bearing to suit.

Commander Oliver's daughter, Miss Nan Oliver, said there was not a word in her father's memoirs about the condition of the engine room when the ship was brought to a halt.

Word of mouth has it that there was a complete loss of power, including, of course, lighting. Captain Arliss's action on the bridge averted immediate death and destruction; my father and his stokers, working in the dark and confusion, got the ship moving, and made it possible for her and her human cargo to reach safe haven.

Once *Napier* was repaired she took part in a number of runs to help supply the garrison at Tobruk. These were known as 'Spud Runs'. Commander Oliver described an incident which occurred during one of these trips.

About half way along the main deck of destroyers there used to be a steel superstructure supporting a four-barrelled pom-pom gun and enclosing the two circular hatches to the engine room. And between the hatches was a wooden bench, unofficially called the Engineer's Bridge. A destroyer chief would spend hours here at sea in the Med, it being the best location from which to proceed promptly forward, or aft, or below.

In the 1940s many engineer officers, including me, had taken to wearing white overalls instead of the brown jean garments customary up to that time. I had observed that many destroyer officers had their stripes of rank painted on the front of their tin hats, to facilitate recognition in the dust and smoke of battle, but decided it was unnecessary for me.

There came a time when certain Australian troops in Tobruk were relieved by Polish units; thus our 'return cargo' one night was a company of Tobruk-tired but quite fit AIF infantry. And having been below while manoeuvring away from the wharf, I came up the ladder to the engineer's bridge—and found it occupied by a large soldier and his kit. He had managed to slip away from his blue-torch sailor guide and perch in a very cushy spot.

Not having the heart to send him forward, I said, 'Move over, Digger. There's room for two.' 'Righto mate,' said he, and moved his clobber enough to let me sit beside him. And so we yarned away the middle watch and swapped views on many things. And his views on some subjects were very set.

I sympathised with soldiers having to live in the dirt and discomfort of Tobruk, remarking that we were much better off in feeding and washing facilities. But my friend disagreed. 'I like firm earth under me. You can have your Navy.' And he disliked Pommies. 'But,' said I, 'aren't all your artillery men in Tobruk British units, and aren't they pretty hot stuff?' Then he gave me his opinion of officers—any officers, military, naval, etc. Apparently they were the bottom of the barrel. I said what I could in defence of these warriors, pointing out that most officers most of the time tried to do their best.

In those days, British warships at sea used to close up at General Quarters (Action Stations) five minutes before dawn and dusk, and stay there for 10 or 15 minutes until full daylight or dark prevailed—to avoid being tricked or trapped in the dicey light conditions just before and after sunrise and sunset.

On this occasion, during the dawn stand to my chief engine room artificer poked his head up the engine room hatch and reported something about the port main engine— and addressed me as 'Sir'. And a few minutes later, after dispersal from GQs, [General Quarters] my office messenger and cabin hand stoker, Gardiner, brought me a welcome cup of tea from the after galley, and called me 'Sir'. Whereupon my soldier friend, with rising suspicion in his voice, asked 'Just what are you in this ship?'

'Well, I'm the engineer officer of the ship and staff engineer to Captain (D) 7th Flotilla,' I said. His jaw fell open and 'Jeese,' he exploded, 'I thought you was the cook!' So, next day, in harbour, my winger, Gardiner, acquired brushes and paint and adorned my 'tin 'at' with three stripes.

The weather was mostly fine and clear, but occasionally it played up. This occurred during one Spud Run on which we took to Tobruk some Polish soldiers. With the ship reacting to rough weather the way destroyers do, many of these poor devils were terribly seasick. A few even lost their rifles overboard, and when a soldier does that, he is pretty far gone. But with calmer weather as we neared Tobruk they recovered strongly, and marched away from the wharf singing! Singing on going in to Tobruk! It nearly stopped us unloading.

'Bug' Oliver had entered the Royal Australian Naval College, then at Jervis Bay, in 1917 as a cadet. He was sent to England in 1923 for training in marine engineering and remained in the RAN until 1959. He died on 9 July 1986, aged 83.

Supplied by Nan Oliver of New South Wales

'IT REALLY WAS A TERRIBLE DAY'

Sister Sylvia Duke
6th Australian General Hospital, Australian Imperial Force
Greece 1941

S ylvia Duke and Sophie Healy were good friends and colleagues. So, when Sylvia was posted abroad as a Sister in the 6th Australian General Hospital in Greece, it was only natural they should stay in touch.

Sylvia Duke was enjoying her time in Greece. It was hard work with long hours at the hospital, but the lovely warm sun shining on the mimosa reminded the nurses of the wattle back home, even if it did make them a touch homesick.

And to top it off there were the 'exquisite relics of the ancient Greeks, the ruins of beautiful old temples and amphitheatres, lovely arches—the wonderful Acropolis,' she wrote in a detailed seven-page letter to Sophie.

> Oh Sophie my dear, you would have to see it all to really believe such beauty existed and to truly appreciate it.

But war is no respecter of beauty, and Sylvia was faced each day with treating the wounded under appalling conditions as the fighting grew ever closer to her hospital.

> My dear, I can truly say that from the very first day of our arrival there we never had one full night's rest. We had air raids every night and day. We got so used to wearing our tin hats and even taking them to bed with us.

She was upset at the apparent lack of air support for the troops.

> Sophie dear, those crowds and crowds of our own marvellous lads all so confident and full of fun, sure that before very long we would be in Berlin, if only they had support.

Sister Sylvia Duke.

Oh where were those aeroplanes. I know the RAF did magnificent work before we went into action but this is such a war of action we must have planes to keep pushing forward.

My dear, those days we spent nursing in a hospital about 14 miles [22 km] out of Athens are just like a nightmare—streams and streams of ambulances bringing our boys back, lack of equipment, lack of foods, not enough hands to really make them even a bit comfortable, the Huns dive bombing & machine gunning the ambulance trains, and the ambulance boys taking eight days even to cover a distance that should normally take a few hours—wounded boys coming to us hungry and very little food to give them, boys in agony and a shortage of drugs only to be given in extreme cases. No forceps to do dressings, no sterile dressings even rolls of gauze and cotton wool. There was no advance dressing station ahead. The boys came back with just field dressings on their wounds in their torn and bloody uniforms, unwashed for many days and then if they had the good fortune to have a sponge, their intense gratitude and 'Gee oh Sister, that's great' and 'fancy seeing an Aussie girl too!' and my dear their sigh of relief to have their boots taken off after being on for weeks—Sophie dear, some of those lads were so badly knocked about , such awful wounds and they were all so brave.

I thanked God many times for the privilege of being born an Australian. They had such guts—they could always see another lad who was worse than they themselves—and then my dear the awful sensation of helplessness, that awful hopelessness when evacuation was imminent—we nurses were put on trucks and sent off down to the water front—matron and about 25 other Sisters were on a truck ahead of us. They were boarded on a hospital ship but we arrived at the docks in the midst of an air raid, and as the planes were dive bombing the harbour they cut the ships ropes and away she went leaving the remainder of us on shore. We returned to our former hospital and attempted to carry on—the casualties still pouring in every hour of every day.

We were on movement orders, we did our nursing in our outdoor uniforms expecting our orders to walk out any minute—our nights were passed in empty houses—no beds or any such luxuries and believe me those tiled floors can be jolly hard to sleep on. And then my dear, when our next orders came to go once more—the boys saying 'Cheerio Sister, thanks so much. Hurry up—Go.'

Sophie dear, how it hurt to go and leave them there and then my dear once more army trucks and we were on our way, leaving all our gear behind, taking just what we could carry in our hands—and the Huns so close behind. We arrived late in the day at our rendezvous and spent the remainder of the day in a barley field with enemy planes overhead and then the appalling news that we could not continue any further by rail as first intended. The railroad had been bombed away.

Oh the anxiety of those men for our safety. They then arranged our transport in huge trucks by road—and then a nightmare drive over the mountains through the blackness of the night with no headlights, treachery on every side. Fifth Columnists breaking into our convoy and attempting to stop us—the boys clearing the road of obstructions every little while for us to proceed, shooting out headlights with their revolvers, driving at reckless pace around pot holes in the roads that had sheer drops down to the sea. The awful sense of complete desolation everywhere and the welcome daylight really brought no relief.

We breakfasted on the roadside on tinned bully beef & dry biscuits with no cutlery, just our fingers. We had nothing to drink, only the water in our water bottles—and then on again—enemy planes overhead. The convoy stopped. We left our trucks and scattered running for cover into barley fields, lying face downwards hugging mother earth and wishing our tin hats were somewhat bigger to cover more of us. We spent all the day there. There was small cemetery nearby and we camped among the headstones all day. It really was amazing to see the girls, and the boys too, lying flat down on their faces as the planes flew over us machine gunning on & off all day—between while we ate still iron rations but we boiled our billy on the tomb stones and had a cup of tea. Sophie it really was a terrible day—then with the night, on our way again to complete our nightmare journey.

An air raid was in progress but we continued on in the blackness of the night to a port way down south of Greece [Navplion]; when we finally reached there we had about a mile & a half's walk from the trucks to small boats & we had to carry all our gear. It got heavier every step of the way and girl after girl began discarding even the few possessions she had carried so far. Anything went in our endeavour to lighten weight. At last we board the small boats and out across the black harbour past burning ships that seemed to illuminate a huge area around them, and then alongside a destroyer and then being pulled up on board—big eager sailor's hands. Oh it was marvellous that haven—a supreme sense of security. At last we felt safe. The Navy would look after us now. Now we could sit down and rest.

And then the great discovery it was an Australian destroyer [HMAS *Voyager*]. The crew went mad not knowing their passengers were to be Sisters, they had expected to get troops aboard and when they discovered we were Australian girls they hugged us tight. We were all so tired. I slept that night under the dining room table in the Officer's Mess with about eight others. The girls just went to sleep wherever they dropped and we put to sea. The morning sunlight disclosed girls everywhere, sleeping on the wet decks, under the Ak Ak guns, in corridors, every cabin handed over to us. The whole ship was ours for a few hours while they took us to safety on a small island.

During the morning the guns brought down one plane and the noise was deafening—but my dear, they delivered us safely and then we worked again on the island amongst our evacuated casualties until we were again, after about four days, sent on to Alexandria. But my dear, the shortage of everything on the island was appalling.

I will tell you all about our sojourn there perhaps by the next mail.

When Sylvia Duke returned home, she married an Army officer before moving to Victoria.

Supplied by Sophie Healy of New South Wales

'I HOPE I NEVER HAVE TO LIVE THROUGH ANOTHER DAY LIKE TODAY'

Able Seaman Harry Dale
HMAS *Karangi,* Royal Australian Navy
Darwin 19 February 1942

The day the Japanese bombed Darwin is one that Harry Dale will never forget. He was on a ship in the harbour when the planes began their raid on Thursday 19 February 1942, and was lucky to survive.

Harry Dale had joined HMAS *Karangi* while it was still being fitted out at Cockatoo Dock in Sydney. The small ship had two strange-looking steel horns protruding from the bow, as it was to be a boom defence vessel in Darwin Harbour.

HMAS *Karangi* left Sydney on 26 December 1941 and headed up the east coast, stopping briefly in Townsville and arriving in Darwin early in January 1942. The next few weeks were spent settling into the work of working on the 'trotts' of the boom gates. A trott is a panel between each flotation barrel made up of stretcher weights and mesh that were only open in daylight hours so Japanese submarines couldn't slip into the harbour undetected.

Word came through that a convoy had been attacked by Japanese planes and on 18 February between 20 and 30 ships steamed into Darwin Harbour including USS *Houston*, HMAS *Swan*, HMAS *Warrego* and USS *Peary*. As dusk closed in, USS *Houston* sailed back out through the boom gates heading west towards Fremantle.

Harry Dale decided he would keep a record of his time in Darwin. Because it was strictly forbidden to keep a diary or to tell any family member anything about the war, Harry hit on the idea of writing letters to his mother—but not posting them. Thus he kept a record of events that included a vivid description of the bombing of Darwin.

> The time is near 2400 hours (midnight). What a day; boy, I'll never forget today, a lot has happened in a short time. I'll try and keep this up to date, just in case any thing happens. The ship has now stopped, we are now laying a fair way up the East arm at

---

Able Seaman Harry Dale in summer uniform.

anchor, I don't know how far we have come, but here we are, I'll try and fill in the details as they happened, here goes.

Cecil Dobell and I were on duty this morning, just before 1000. We were up on the gun deck together, just skulking around, and having a smoke. Cec was oiling the breach of the gun. The *Karangi* has a 12 pounder Ack Ack gun and two Hispano machine guns. The Hispanos are located on the wings of the bridge. I think they were left over from the last war, still they work OK. Anyway, we heard this low droning sound. It was a plane but sounded pretty high up. Then it came into view, it wasn't one, but many. They all glistened silver in the sun, like they were painted with silver frost. It was the sun shining on them. It looked like nine, then another nine, then another nine. They could have been altogether, they were flying in arrow head formation, with one leader. I said to Cec 'they're not ours'. Cec said 'they're Japs, we don't own that many.'

By now they were well into view coming across the harbour in a line, which to me was taking them straight up the town. We reckon they were 30,000 feet high. I raced into the wheel house and pressed the alarm button, then I stood in the doorway. As they got closer I could see their bombs starting to fall. All the planes let them go together. They looked like golf balls.

I watched them right down to the ground. The first bomb to hit looked as if it hit between the signal station and the ships tied up alongside the wharf. I looked at the ship's clock—it was showing 0958 hours (two minutes to 10 am). That's one time I shouldn't forget. About the same time as it hit the wharf, I know there is a ship there unloading depth charges [*Neptuna*]. I'd say it copped a hit. By now our gun crews have closed up and the crew are all at action stations. We were a little lucky—our anchor was not on the anchor cable but on a 'brake slip stopper', which meant we didn't have to use up any steam to raise it. We were able to slip the lot into the harbour. That's where it is now. You can see all the ships belching out smoke as the stokers are really stoking the boilers right up, trying to get up a head of steam quickly so they can get under way. The old HMAS *Platypus* is at anchor between us and the wharf. I don't think she will be able to get under way—she is used as a supply ship, has never been moved since we have been here. If those depth charges blow the old *Platypus* will be very lucky to stay afloat. She is not that far away from the wharf.

The dive bombers are now in action. The USS *Peary*, who is only a few hundred yards away from us on our port quarter, is putting up plenty of flack and machine gun fire. There is a small cloud just above her. There are five dive bombers. They seem to be hidden in the cloud. They are dropping every thing at her. Our little 12 pounder is going great, haven't hit any thing yet. We made the tail of one of the dive bombers wobble, it must be out of bombs and ammo as it has flown right at and over us and kept going.

My job on the gun is to set the fuses and keep the ammo up. The magazine is under the mess deck. Ken Trayhurn is down there loading them into a canvas bag. Spud Murphy hauls them up, then runs along the deck, hands them up to me on the gun deck. The *Peary* has just been hit again. She is on fire. She never managed to get up any speed before she got hit again. The ships along side the wharf have just blown up, can't see the old *Platypus*. I think she must be gone.

We have all ducked for cover, shrapnel is falling everywhere. The *Manunda*, the hospital ship, is only a few hundred yards off our port bow. Here comes a Kittyhawk, its belly light is flashing 'dot dash' all the time. There's a bloody Zero after the Kitty. The Nip is firing all guns. They have just hopped over the *Manunda* (looks like the *Manunda* was strafed by the Nip as he flew past). The Kitty is headed straight along our port side. I can see the Hispano on the port side working, bullets are flying every where. The Japs' bullets are raking along the *Karangi's* side. I'm hiding behind a stanchion. The Jap planes have disappeared. The bridge calls down to see if anyone is injured. All on the gun deck are present, some one yells, 'where's Murphy'. He bobs up out of the winch house. Don't hold out much hope for the Kitty pilot.

We are under way. The *Zealander* is astern of the *Manunda* and has been hit. She is ablaze down the stern, big fire. They are taking to the life boat. We are heading toward them. They are rowing toward the *Manunda*. Looks like a direct hit on the *Peary's* magazine, OH!! She has blown sky high. What an explosion. We have copped the full force of the blast. I've got bells in my ears. She's sinking stern first. Nearly under now. The forward turret is still firing. We are pumping shells out as fast as we can. I can see the form of a sailor right on top of the blast. The *Peary* is nearly under. Can see another life boat being rowed away from the wharf. Don't know how they have survived. The old *Platypus* is still afloat. We are still firing at anything our gun can reach. The boys yell out the setting they want and I set to that. We can't get over 12,000 to 15,000 feet in height. It's useless wasting ammo trying to reach the high level bombers. We are just fending off any low level fighters or dive bombers that are around 1000 feet or less.

The Catalinas went with one run of bombs. They have sunk the lot. There's a torpedo bomber carrying a great big torpedo under its belly. It's keeping out of the way. Reckon they expected to find the USS *Houston*. Bloody glad she got away yesterday, Where ever you look there are burning or sinking ships, the air is filled with the smell of cordite, gun fire, and exploding bombs. There are still explosions going on. The bombers haven't let up. We are making way towards the boom gate, probably only four or five knots. The town looks to have some big fires. The shore ack ack are still trying to reach the high level planes. Don't reckon they have any hope. The worst seems to have passed. Hope they don't come back. No one on our ship has been hit, we certainly have been lucky, especially when that Zero chased the Kitty along our port side. I reckon by the time they had sunk the *Peary* the dive bombers were out of bombs. Can't imagine why they would have left us without letting at least one or two sticks go, as we were certainly firing at them.

Can't see or hear any more planes. We are heading toward the boom gate, just passed two ships—all that is showing is their super structure above the water. No crew to be seen, plenty of wreckage. We are now out at the boom gate. Seems a fighter was going past the gate ship when it turned about and started strafing it. One seaman badly injured, a chap named Pony Moore. They have managed to get him headed for the *Manunda*.

The time is 1215 hours. We can hear planes, we are under way again as evidently there is nothing we can do here. The Japs are now bombing what looks like the RAAF base. They are in a wave of 27, flying in arrow head formation. Looks like it's the same pattern as this morning. We have a good view from here, as we watch the bombs explode. Here comes another wave of 27. The first wave has flown out over the harbour, turned before they reached us and are now heading north. Lucky for us there doesn't seem to be any fighters with them. The other wave has just unloaded their bombs, and headed north. Can't see any more, there mustn't be any thing left of the RAAF base.

The aftermath of the bombing.

We are now heading back to where we were this morning. As we get nearer to the boom wharf, it's been about four hours since the Japs made their first raid, we have been going over to each ship that's sunk looking for survivors. They have either got away in the life boats, been trapped in their hulls, or are floating about with the wreckage. The harbour is littered with debris of all sorts. Can see a few ships in the distance. Like us, they are still afloat. All the crew are still closed up at action stations. The magazines are full of shells, so I gather it's wait and see what happens. Still a few hours till dusk. Can't come soon enough for me. None of us on the gun deck have any idea where we are headed. Seems we are about to enter the East arm. No idea where that goes. We are now proceeding at a very reduced rate of knots. At the moment I'm not needed on the gun crew. They have plenty of ammo. Roy Stone, he's the Bosun, has got me to heave the lead, that means I heave a line which has a seven pound lead weight on the end. I call out how deep the water is using the different markings on the line—so many fathoms deep, so the skipper knows how much water is under the ship so we don't run aground.

I have been relieved a couple of times, Cecil Dobell is doing it now. I have come down to the mess for a cup of kai (hot chocolate). The engines seem to have stopped. On deck I see Nobby Clarke. He is a PO/Stoker—seems we are stopping here for the night. Well, that takes care of Thursday 19 February 1942 as it is nearly 2400 hours. I hope I never have to live through another day like today.

Supplied by Harry Dale of Victoria

'OUR GOVERNMENT HAD SOLD THEM THE SCRAP IRON, BUT THEY BROUGHT IT BACK!'

Driver Rex Ruwoldt
19th Light Horse (Machine Gun) Regiment
Darwin 1942

R ex Ruwoldt was just 17 when he enlisted in 1940. Officially he was too young but a little adjustment to his date of birth fixed that problem.

He trained to be a machine-gunner in army camps in Hamilton and Bendigo. He then went to an armoured school where he earned licenses to drive all forms of army transport, from motor bikes to tanks.

He was posted to Darwin and arrived there early in January 1942 as a member of the 19th Light Horse (Machine Gun) Regiment. By then he was 18 years old.

> We didn't have any horses. We didn't have much of anything else either, so I was a Bren Gun Carrier driver without a Bren Gun Carrier. We went first to Winnellie for two weeks, then to man the two concrete machine gun posts between Lee Point and Leanyah Creek.

> At that time that area was covered with rain forest which was full of mossies, spiders as big as your hand, and scorpions as big as crayfish. We fed them all. We had 1000 mossies per man, and we knew every one by name. Some of them were big enough to shake you by the hand.

> Grass fires were another problem. The RAAF pilot who delivered the daily *Army News* paper had great difficulty finding the camps, so when he found one, he fired his Very pistol into the dry grass. After that, he was able to navigate from one black patch to the next.

> The only bathing facilities were with the crocodiles in Leanyah Creek, or with the blue bottles in the surf. The road from Darwin to Lee Point was a single lane gravel

Rex Ruwoldt, Vic Schumann and Allen Ruwoldt.

track; there was no road from Lee Point to Leanyah Creek, so we had to build one with picks, shovels and an axe.

Rex Ruwoldt's sub-unit, 11 Platoon, consisted of 28 men who were given the task of defending one kilometre or more of beach against an invasion by possibly 20,000 Japanese soldiers.

They could have landed their tanks on the beach in front of us and gone right through us. In the event of an invasion, we were to delay the enemy until reinforcements could be brought up. It would have been a short delay, we only had ammunition for 5 minutes!

When the first raid started I was in the scrub between Lee Point and Leanyah Creek. A Zero dived and fired a burst at an American Kittyhawk which was right in line with me. The bullets ripped through the trees over my head and I suddenly learnt how to hit the deck and flatten myself out to the thickness of a piece of cardboard without even thinking about it.

Their Vickers guns were set in concrete pill-boxes pointing out to sea and were useless in an air raid as they couldn't be raised more than about 20 degrees above the horizon.

It was pretty devastating to watch the carnage over Darwin and not be able to do anything about it.

After the raid, everyone expected a landing to be made at any time, so they waited. Guard duty was two hours on, four hours off, so they did not get much sleep.

At 0300 one morning there was a red alert. There were enemy ships seven miles [11 km] out, so it was every man to his post. There was nobody hundreds of yards either side of Lee Point, so Les Sudholz and I crept quietly out along the track to keep watch at the Point. We met no Japs, but it was so dark that I got within three feet [less than 1 m] of a kangaroo which jumped suddenly out of the bushes and frightened hell out of both of us.

Most of their food supplies had been destroyed in the raid and they were reduced to half rations for about two months.

What with little food and the mossies sucking the life out of us we led a pretty lousy existence and lost a lot of weight.

They were dangerous days. It was even more dangerous if you were as accident prone as one of my mates. He accidentally fired his rifle inside a concrete pill box; knocked a chunk of concrete out of the ceiling. He dived for the door, said it was a good job he got out before the ricochet got him! Later he was posted to New Guinea where he blew up a cookhouse. His wife told me she wrote to the army for a copy of his army record; she wanted to find out which side he was really on!

Towards the end of March, Rex's unit was moved to the RAAF base on ground defences.

We finally got some Bren gun carriers, but on Anzac Day we copped 84 bombs and one hit my carrier.

The bombs were mostly 'Daisy Cutters'—anti personnel bombs filled with shrapnel. They had a rod on the nose so they exploded above ground level blasting shrapnel in all directions.

My carrier was dug in about 75 cm below ground level, and I was in a slit trench nearby with my carrier crew. Two daisy cutters dropped 16 metres apart; one 6 metres one way, the other 10 metres the other way; we were in the middle. The shock and the pain in the ears from the blast was horrendous.

There wasn't a blade of grass left in the area. Everything above ground in the area was shredded, including my underwear; fortunately I wasn't wearing them at the time. I had washed them and hung them out to dry. After the raid we picked up shrapnel including bolts branded 'Ajax' (McPhersons), 'MH' (Massey Harris) and 'S' (Singer). Our Government had sold them the scrap iron, but they brought it back!

One bomb set fire to an anti-tank truck and ammunition, and the explosions continued for another 2 hours and we had to keep our heads down.

Two Americans passing in a Jeep were killed.

Three of our fellows had a daisy cutter hit only three feet from their slit trench, but the blast went over their heads, and they survived with burst ear drums and severe shock. Two of them have since passed on, the third gradually came out of a coma in hospital three days later, temporarily deaf but as his vision gradually returned he could see ghostly white figures floating around the ward. 'Christ', he thought, 'they must be angels! I've really bought it this time!'

The official record of the raid said: 'There were no injuries and little damage.' The bombings continued and we lived a boring frustrated existence in miserable conditions until the end of 1943. The diet was sadly deficient in essential vitamins and nearly everyone suffered badly from tropical ulcers, tinea, and prickly heat.

The forces at Darwin were determined to keep the Japanese from gaining a foothold on the Australian mainland should they attempt an invasion.

Supplied by Rex Ruwoldt of Victoria

'MAY YOU SOON COME BACK TO US ALL'

Daisy (Annie) Boyden
Civilian
Randwick, NSW 1942

When Singapore fell to the Japanese in February 1942, almost 15,000 Australian troops were taken prisoner. Families back home waited anxiously for news of their loved ones, desperate to know if they had been killed in the fighting or had become prisoners of war. Many waited in vain. Details of casualties were spasmodic and mail from those in captivity was almost non-existent.

Daisy Boyden was devastated by the disappearance of her son, Arthur, who had been in Singapore during the Japanese invasion. She had no idea if he was still alive but decided to hope for the best and continued to write regular letters to him.

She was advised of a forwarding address for Arthur but the letters she sent to Singapore were never delivered and were eventually returned. Then she was told not to send any more until she received news of Arthur's whereabouts. But she kept writing the letters without posting them, and this helped keep her optimistic.

Daisy was a highly religious woman and peppered her letters with quotes from the Bible, such as 'God helped him ... He was marvellously helped. 2 Chron 26.7.15.'

A letter, dated 25 January 1942, in response to one received from Arthur, written while he was still in Malaya, was full of hope and described a family outing.

> We all slept well, of course. I wake up very often through the night and pray for you, & the dear children say their prayers after our prayer. It is just lovely hearing them pray their prayer for you after their usual 'Jesus tender shepherd hear me.'
>
> I let Dai [Arthur's wife] have your letter and she sent it back with Beverley [Arthur's daughter]. She was very interested and we think your suggestion very good, passing

Arthur and Dai Boyden.

on letters to one another. I copy those I get into my 'War letter book'. I think of you day and night and I commit you into God's special keeping and I know He will keep you and surround you with His mercy and loving kindness.

A few days later, she wrote again upon hearing that the British had blown the causeway between Malaya and Singapore to prevent the Japanese from crossing.

What a lot you will have to tell us when you write. We are putting our whole trust in God, knowing that He is able to help & supply all you need.

I hope you got my letter and the children's we sent last mail dear. I will put down here what I sent in the parcel: 1 Johnson's powder, box of muscatel raisins, Jordan almonds, 2 books, *Hayes Nook* and *Sweik*, 1 pair khaki cotton socks, Log Cabin fine cut tobacco, 4 pkts cigarette papers, pkt safety razors, cake of Erasmus soap and powder puff.

On 5 February she wrote again when Dai had received a cable from Arthur in Singapore.

What a joy we had when Dai received your cable from Singapore. She phoned me and with such a thankful heart. I passed on the message to each member of the family. Stewart [Arthur's older brother], I could hear the tears in his voice when he said 'thank God'.

Much love from us all, specially from your loving and devoted mother. I have never once missed writing to you since you left, each week. 'The angel of the Lord encampeth around about them that fear Him and delivereth them.' I have 102 names on my prayer list and pray for each one separately every morning and all thanks to God, they have been kept safe through the love of Jesus.

Her next letter described the 'most anxious and terrible week' knowing what the troops were going through in Singapore.

What awful suffering. I can scarcely bear to read it & yet feel I cannot miss a word.

This morning we went to the 11 o'clock Holy Communion Service, Paul [another brother] & I. How earnestly we pray for you and Lance [another brother] there.

St Jude's looks so strange. Each Sunday, while the people are in church, two wardens are in the tower, i.e. in the gallery. There is a little blue light fixed so that directly there is a raid coming, the blue light flashes out so that Mr Abrahams can see it. He then asks everyone to stand, telling them a raid is coming & he just pronounces the benediction & the congregation goes out in sections so there can be no crowding. They are to be 'cool, calm and collected'.

There are four large cards painted in scarlet: Area 1, Area 2, Area 3 and Area 4 and we know which entrance we have to leave the Church, Paul & I by No 2 Area door.

On 22 February, after the fall of Singapore, Daisy Boyden wrote about how worried they all were for Arthur. It was at this stage she was advised not to post any more letters.

> We do not expect to hear just yet, but we are not to send any more parcels or letters to S [Singapore] but I will be writing each week and I expect they will all be taken care of for you and you will get them in a heap.

The next week she wrote again.

> It seems so strange to write a letter to you and not be able to send, but I am going to write a few lines every Sunday, hoping when we hear where you are, we will be able to send all our back letters by air mail, if we put by the 9d, so that you get them as soon as possible.

> This will be the last letter I will be writing to you from our dear little flat as we find in these days we cannot keep it up. But we are not moving from Randwick, in fact, only 10 minutes walk from where we are.

> We have taken a large room on the ground floor which will do for a bed-sitting room for me, and Paul has a small bedroom next to mine and we are going to board. The house is a large kindergarten school but all the children have been evacuated to the country until after the war.

> Oh Arthur darling, if I had not committed you into God's keeping and trusting in the name of Jesus I could not go on, but I believe God will bring you back again, after all you must have gone through.

She wrote on 8 March following the move.

> The address above will show you we have left the dear home flat. We arrived here last Friday, March 6. Dear Stewart and Queen kindly came and called for me at Avoca Street & brought me in the car. It was such a help & Paul had come with a man to have the furniture put in the right place to look as much like home as possible.

The following week found her feeling more positive.

> Another week gone, one nearer to your homecoming. Oh what a day it will be. I'm not going to write you any more long letters because when I read them over, I think you will be weary—so I will try to condense the news.

> We have not been able to find a place for everything yet; they are put into a shed as we unpack. It is so nice to have Lil and the girls walking about overhead. [Arthur's sister, Lilien, had taken the flat above Daisy's room.] Every man, woman and child has to register their name, their duties, their age, what they would be willing to do in war work. Lil has offered for munition work part of the day. That is for married women who also have domestic duties. Alice is on the switchboard at the university

several nights a week; she gets very tired but loves the work. Helen is at war work at her position.

The lack of news was now beginning to tell.

This silence between us is very hard to bear, but we must be brave & patient until we get word from each other. I am still writing each week to keep you in touch with all that has happened since we said goodbye.

We are getting more settled but the meals here are dreadfully haphazard—I've not had anything since my tomato juice and milk, which I had before Paul left. I am simply longing for a cup of tea which I expected at 11; it is now 12.37. I am dreadful complaining when perhaps you have nothing to eat or drink (may God forgive me).

On 6 April she wrote about attending church for the Easter service.

We all went to St Jude's & had a lovely communion service. The Rector was so reverent and seemed to feel every word he said.

Paul's case at the Military Court comes off next Friday. He applied for exemption on account of my health and we are praying God to guide him.

Paul's case with the Military Court was the subject of her next letter on 12 April. It was her eighth since the fall of Singapore.

His case was put off for a fortnight but he said the Magistrate seemed favourable. The doctor had given him a certificate to say what I was suffering from & my age & he stated that it would be very detrimental to my health if he was taken from me. Of course, dear, we are making it a matter of prayer.

Her next letter was on 26 April.

Yesterday being dear Dagma's [Dai's] birthday, Paul rang her up to know if it would be convenient for him to come up & bring our gifts. She had promised to go to No 9 for lunch & they asked her to bring Paul with her, which she did, & later on in the afternoon, she, Paul, Beverley and Ian [Arthur's son] came to see us all. Oh my dear one, how you must long to see them all again, please God it will be soon.

You will be glad to know Paul got his exemption from military service—oh I am so glad. Being 43 and in the NES, the court said they would grant his request.

It was Arthur's birthday on 30 April.

I am going to send a cable of enquiry to the Red Cross, because by the *SMH* I see they are able to send an enquiry cable (only a few at a time) to find out about dear ones who are in Japanese hands.

There were a list of names of civilians and prisoners in yesterday's *SMH*. The lists are being released today through the International Red Cross in Geneva, more lists to be released soon. Inquiries for servicemen & prisoners-of-war. I do pray through this we may hear good news of you my dear one.

The next few letters were mostly sad news of people ill or dying, but one bright note was the visit of Arthur's daughter, Beverley.

Beverley found her way from No 9 Springfield Avenue to our house. Freda put her on the train.

Her stomach is a bit upset so we could not go to church this morning. I was so disappointed but never mind. Better luck next time. She looks such a lady in her new coat and hat. She is growing quite tall.

On 4 June she wrote again.

We all thought of you on your 12th wedding day. I do pray that you both may have a very happy anniversary for the next.

I had four of my letters I had written to you returned to me. I did feel sad they never got to you. One had a letter from Beverley and Ian enclosed but I am saving them all to go in the packet I am sending you when we can get them through to you.

On 21 June 1942, Daisy Boyden wrote what turned out to be her last letter to Arthur. She was saddened by the death of her closest friend, Mrs Chick.

I shall feel her loss very much but she suffered so much in her last year of life—we can only thank God for taking her over the other side.

I am writing this in bed dear, so you will excuse the cramped letters dear heart. All your brothers and sister and sisters-in-law, nieces and nephews enquire after you and send love. May you soon come back to us all.

Daisy's health continued to deteriorate and she was confined to bed. The death of Mrs Chick, and the heartache of not knowing what had happened to Arthur, all contributed to her end. She died on 1 December 1943, aged 79.

But her prayers must have been answered, for Arthur survived being a prisoner of war, despite being forced to work on the infamous Burma–Thailand railway, and returned to Australia at the end of the war.

Supplied by Beverley Boyden of Queensland

'THE MOST WONDERFUL NEWS WE HAVE EVER HAD'

John Peters
Civilian
Muchea, Western Australia 1941–1945

John Peters was a retired schoolteacher who owned the general store in Muchea, a small town 54 km north of Perth. He spent a great deal of time listening to the radio during World War II. But the programs he tuned in to on his short wave set were not for his own entertainment. Pete, as he was known since his days with the 3rd Field Ambulance at Gallipoli, was trying to find out what had become of his son, John, who had gone missing at the fall of Singapore.

So he listened each night to the mocking voice of 'Tokyo Rose' as she announced details of Australians captured by the Japanese. He realised that a good many other people similarly would be worried about missing relatives, so he began to make a note of the names mentioned by Tokyo Rose and passed on news to others. He also discovered other frequencies where this information was available.

> Early in the piece I recognised, and very soon had definite proof, that these messages were authentic enough as far as letting people know their loved ones were at least alive.

He kept meticulous records of names and the times and dates of broadcasts and referred to them when people began writing to him as a source of information on missing relatives. His wife, Blanche, and daughter, Joan, worked with him.

> Although our self-imposed task has been most exacting and very often greatly inconvenient—we have not missed a session that we knew about—and there are nine of these a day now.

Joan recalls helping her parents, listening each night to 'Tokyo Rose' and others.

> I used to find her voice very galling. She had an aggravating, mocking tone of voice but we soon got used to it.

The General Store at Muchea.
John Peters as a young man.

As he listened to 'Tokyo Rose' and others, Pete would scribble down on precious pieces of paper the names of soldiers and any messages that might have been relayed. First he would attempt to contact the soldiers' families by telephone. He would also check the phone book for addresses. If he found any, he could send on news and messages by putting the envelopes directly into the open mailbag of the train at Muchea station, which stopped each night between 1 am and 3 am.

If he was unable to locate a phone number or address—and there were not many people who had telephones during the war—he would ring up the local police station to pass on the information.

> We were fortunate in having one of the really good short wave radio sets for the job and the fact that most of my work is at home—I am storekeeper here—and without these two conditions it would not be done.

Pete used old ledgers, journals, circulars and any other pieces of paper he could lay his hands on. His daughter Joan recalls that paper was scarce and much valued during the war.

> Everybody saved paper and envelopes for him.

Many people who received the notes would write back to thank him enclosing a stamp to help pay for the cost, while others donated small amounts of money and urged him to keep up the service.

All the time he continued these endeavours, he was hoping to hear about his own missing son but it wasn't until November 1945 that he finally learned John had been killed in the fall of Singapore.

Meanwhile, hundreds of families received news of their loved ones thanks to Pete's voluntary service. Joan has a collection of 820 letters sent by grateful families from all over Australia.

> Your letter of the 8th regarding my son, Phil, caused a thrill to many homes. I had heard from the Department of the Army about two weeks ago that my lad was a prisoner of war in Malaya, but the other boys mentioned, namely Gregor McDonald, Halwin Buttsworth and Bill Bell, had not been heard of, so you can imagine the joy amongst the families of those three boys when we phoned them the contents of your letter.

Another letter from a grateful mother read in part:

> I wish to express to you my sincere thanks and gratitude for your kindness in sending on the message, which you heard last night from Saigon, sent by my son of whom I have had no tidings since the fall of Singapore. You can just imagine how thankful

I was to get the message, which the local constable gave within a few minutes of receiving it from you.

News of a missing son prompted this mother to write:

It gave us untold pleasure to know that our dear one was safe & well, & feel that you are doing a great job in letting relatives know of these letters.

And another mother was ecstatic at hearing news:

I received your most welcome letter yesterday (28-8-43) & it is the most wonderful news we have ever had. Yes, that is our soldier son XX36828 Gnr L.H. Howell. The last letter we had from him was 27th Jan 1942 from Malaya since then silence, but the news you have sent us is wonderful news & we are all overjoyed by it.

Many wives learned from Pete that husbands were still alive as POWs:

I was delighted to receive your letter today and words cannot express my feelings when I heard the good news of my husband, and to know he is safe and well.

Letters poured in not only from all over Australia but from New Zealand, South Africa, the British Isles and even one from New Guinea.

After the war Pete continued to run his store. Because he spoke four languages he also taught English to the migrants who arrived to work in the timber mill at Muchea. He spent many hours helping them with tax returns, writing their letters and did all the estimates of the acreage cleared for those on farms. He also acquired the local post office to go with his store until Joan and her husband, Wally Edwards, took over the store in 1948. Pete continued with the Post Office for some years but was taken ill with cancer in 1956 and died in 1961.

There are hundreds of families throughout Australia and beyond who have reason to be grateful for the many hours Pete and his family dedicated to distributing news of missing relatives.

Supplied by Joan Edwards of Western Australia

TOUGH ENTRY
REQUIREMENTS FOR THE
LATE ARRIVALS CLUB

Sergeant Observer Reginald Norman 'Mick Ey'
14 Squadron Royal Air Force, 454 Squadron, Royal Australian Air Force
Middle East 1941–1944

Mick Ey could regard himself as unusually fortunate while flying in the Middle East with 454 Squadron. After all, it's not many people who can say they were involved in five crashes and still lived to tell the tale.

He flew in Blenheim and Baltimore bombers operating over the Western Desert from October 1941 until his return to Australia in November 1944.

Mick told his son, Tony Ey, about one crash that resulted in an 11-day trek through the desert for him and his mates before they were rescued.

> It was in the Middle East during March 1942 and as a crew we had just joined 14 Squadron after completing our time in the Operational Training Unit in Kenya. I was the Navigator/Bomb Aimer, Pommy Mills was the Pilot, and Johnny Hunt was the Wireless Operator/Air Gunner.

> On March 16 we took off on a 'Squadron Do' in our old Mk. IV Bristol Blenheim. These were twin-engined bombers and our registration number was *V 5446*. There were nine Blenheims in the formation and we had to fly out across the Libyan desert and into Tripoli to have a crack at a target up there.

> As Pommy recalled: 'Coming back from a bombing raid west of Benghazi we were sailing along for home when our starboard engine began to pack up. We were only a thousand feet at the time. The port engine wasn't giving full power either, so we were done. I kept the aircraft going without any oil pressure at all, and gave the 'duff' engine an extra burst now and again to regain a bit of height.'

Mick Ey left, with Pommy Mills and Johnny Hunt.

We had been flying over German ground troops earlier so we could have copped a stray bullet, although of course we will never know. We knew we had to keep well down into the desert to the south, well away from the German garrisons along the coast.

We decided to jettison as much as we could, as Blenheims were notorious for flying like a brick on one engine and we wanted to get as far as we could. We dumped our bomb load and that helped a bit although we were losing height all the time. We discussed our options as we knew we were definitely going down. The choice was a wheels down landing, or wheels up and belly it in. We all agreed to try a wheels down as the old Blenheim was a pretty slow old bird. When the engine finally seized after about twenty minutes, Pommy feathered the prop.

There was nothing to do except get down as quickly as possible. I turned back into wind on the one engine and decided to do a wheels down landing in case she went up in flames. The country was full of rock shelves and I hadn't had time to pick or choose a suitable spot to bring her down'. As we steadily lost altitude Pommy said, 'Alright, this is it' and we all knew there was only going to be one bite of the cherry—either we made it or we didn't. 'I steered clear of the worst rocks and we came to a standstill with the tail wheel broken off and the prop tips bent as we went over a bit of an escarpment.'

As it happened we couldn't have struck a worse place to land. It was all rocky outcrops, rough as the devil, anyway Pommy did a great job, no doubt about that. He touched her down while trying to heave the aeroplane over the worst of the rocky areas. She banged and bounced and finally she was on the ground for good and as we skidded along, the tail wheel and one of the main wheels was torn off, so one wing was low and this caused her to eventually ground loop. When we came to a halt, the high wing came to rest alongside a large rock outcrop about 6 or 7 feet high so all we had to do was walk along the wing and step off onto the top of this rock. It was an absolute miracle how Pommy managed to land on such rocky ground without injury to any of us.

Being in enemy territory it was useless to wait besides our aircraft, so we decided to walk. We immediately took stock of what we had. We had a water bottle each, a first aid kit, a tin of peaches and a packet of Army ration biscuits.

I removed the aircraft's P6 compass from the pilot's position, ripped a small canvas bag from the inside skin of the aircraft, stripped some shroud line from one of the parachutes and made a little bag to hold the compass. With the shrouds looped around my neck, I could then carry it on my chest. So away we went. We walked for about 4 hours and stopped for our first night at the base of a fairly steep sandhill. It rained that night and hell it got cold too. We shivered all night but it wasn't a normal shiver, our whole bodies quivered with the cold. It was the only night it did rain. Later on we came to pray for rain but nothing happened.

The next morning we got started pretty early because we couldn't sleep much and headed off on a compass course of 045°. The idea was that we wanted to bypass Tobruk as 'Jerry' still controlled it. We had estimated that we were about 180–200 miles [290–320 km] inland.

We walked all day with the occasional spell when we would have a nibble of a biscuit and a bit of water. We knew we had to ration it all out. Our water bottles had corks in them so we decided to ram the corks home in the necks of the bottles so that we couldn't get them out. Each bottle had a pin on a chain and with this we forced a small hole in the cork. To get any water we had to blow through this hole to slightly pressurise the bottle so that when we tipped the bottle up, the pressure forced a few drops of water out. We knew that those few drops were all we could afford to have.

They had their peaches that night with some of the broken biscuits, which were also strictly rationed. Over the first two days and nights they made good progress and covered some 65 km. It wasn't until the third day that they began to realise the seriousness of their position and wondered what their families were thinking, as by now they would have been posted as missing.

The worst part up until then was our flying boots which were wool lined. Our feet just slopped around in them and they played merry hell with our feet. We still had some parachute cord so we tied this around our boots to try and keep the boots tight on our feet. We just seemed to walk and walk. Some nights we would walk until about 8 or 9 o'clock until we found somewhere to camp.

There were no trees, just a little bit of bush called camelthorn and we'd try and find a little bit of a ridge to dig a bit of a hole and fill it with this camelthorn. We'd lie on that but it used to get that bloody cold, your teeth would chatter because we only had a pair of trousers and a shirt each; nothing else.

What we used to do was toss to see who would be in the middle first, and we'd all face the same way so that we could fit in, and we'd stay like that until we got stiff and then righto, over we'd go. The bloke in the middle would get on the outside so we each had a turn being reasonably warm, but some nights were so bloody cold that by about midnight or 1 o'clock in the morning we'd say, 'Come on let's get cracking'.

The compass was luminous so we'd walk a bit at night and towards daylight we'd have a bit of a camp again because we knew we'd be walking all day; and that's how it went on. During the day it was bloody hot but at night it was as cold as charity. The compass only weighed about 6 or 7 pounds [about 3 kg] but it seemed like a half a ton after a while. I had a permanent kink in my neck. On the fourth day we hit a stony plain. You could glimpse the horizon but nothing else—and we kept on seeing mirages. By the fifth day we were out of water.

One night we came on a depression and there had been rain there recently. It was a natural catchment area and there was quite a crop of lucerne growing. Maybe the Italians had planted it. We camped in this patch for the night and it gave us some shelter from the bitterly cold night wind. We were out of water but we found a tortoise. It was bad luck for him because he got knocked on the head. We had no means of cooking so we ate it raw and drank the blood. It was fluid. In the morning we pulled the lucerne between our lips to get the dew. We buried our feet in some moist sand to relieve the pain from our blisters.

Another night we found a British Red Cross pickup that had been knocked out. It was like a utility with a canvas top and had a large red cross on either side. Anyway, that night we decided that we were going to camp in this vehicle. After scratching around inside I found a roll of cotton wool and a tube of Gentian Violet. Our feet were so bad that I said to my mates that I couldn't go any further unless I pricked my blisters and got rid of some of the fluid, even at the risk of them turning septic. So that's what we did and we smeared this Gentian Violet all over our feet, and that eased the pain. That was one of the good nights we had even though there was one hell of a dust storm. Of course next morning when we started to walk, our feet gave us 'what-o'.

One day we spotted some knocked out vehicles, so we walked over to them and we were all scouting around to see what was what. The one I was looking at was an Indian Bren Gun carrier and unfortunately its battery was whacked, otherwise I reckon I could have got it started. Anyway there was nothing I could do about it.

Pommy came over and asked what I'd found. I said, 'Well firstly, there's a 4 gallon tin of Indian curry and it'll burn your insides out, but it's something to eat. I've tried it, and bloody hell it's hot. Another thing, this radiator's got a lot of water in it.'

They found some empty jerry cans and drained the water into them till they ended up with two cans about three-quarters full. It didn't taste too good but it was water and it saved their bacon.

We were determined that we wouldn't part with those jerry cans for anything, so we carried them for about four days I think it was. One bloke in the middle would carry both cans with one either side holding the can as well. When the bloke in the middle was buggered, we would change over.

But I was stuck with that ruddy compass around my neck all the time. It kept us on course and we were right on track when we got picked up. We were aiming for the coast road east of Tobruk and if we knew if we made it, we had a good chance of running into our own troops.

Once we saw a Jerry patrol of three or four vehicles and as we were in a pretty bad way at that stage, we didn't give a bugger who picked us up. We tried to attract their attention but they just sailed by. Probably thought we were bloody wogs.

Much later, in a newspaper interview, Pommy described events.

The mental strain was worse than anything. You don't realise how vivid your imagination can be. In the evening we could see our bar in the mess and all the boys around it. Our eyes began to go to, after about four or five days, and everything became blurred as a result of the glare and sand.

One day they came across some canisters lying around on the ground.

We were pretty fuzzed up by this time; not exactly thinking clearly. These things looked like big thermos flasks and I thought, 'What the hell's this', so I picked one up and had a look at it. It must have been intuition but I thought, 'Hell'. I let it roll off my hand onto the ground as I realised that we had walked right into a bloody German minefield. We quickly backtracked until we were sure we were clear of it.

We hadn't had anything to eat for several days and we had run out of water. Things were getting tough. We were now on our last legs and had given up all hope of getting back alive.

On the tenth day I spotted something in the distance but I couldn't make out what it was, so I said to Pommy and Johnny, 'Let's deviate and go over and see what that is. There might be something to eat.' So we altered course and when we got over there, we found a truck which had been a tanker of some sort. It had been knocked out and was sitting in a deep depression, and down in this depression it looked as though troops had recently been camped there. We were looking for water and thought that there may be a well there, so down we went.

We found three holes in the ground which we thought might contain water. Pommy went to one and I went poking around

Mick Ey at a desert camp.

one of the others. When I got to this particular hole, I found a length of telephone wire which was tied to an old kerosene bucket so I picked up the bucket and sang out to Pommy, 'Hey come here, look at this, there's water in the bucket.'

There was a rock hole which we couldn't see into, but we knew there must be water in it. I said, 'Thank God, we've found some water.' I dropped the bucket down the hole and pulled up about a half a bucket of the best water you've ever tasted in your life. It was crystal clear so we all had a real good slug, and that perked us up quite a bit.

Johnny then said, 'Come over here', and he showed us an area where there had been a lot of troops. It looked like there had been a bit of a fight as there were a lot of empty cartridges and little trenches where someone had obviously dug in. We decided to stay the night there and it occurred to me that the bucket must have been used that morning, as the evaporation rate out there was quite high, and there had been water in the bucket.

I said, 'Someone is not very far away, so we'd better keep an eye open.' Anyway, Johnny walked over to have a good look at the tanker and wedged between the tank and the step which ran around the outside he found a round tin. The label had gone and Johnny was belting it with rocks trying to get it out. He reckoned there was probably something to eat in it. Johnny finally got it out and brought it over to us.

In the meantime, Pommy and I had been scouting around and we rounded up all the little bits of camelthorn that we could find as we intended to have a fire that night. Pommy said there were a lot of cigarette butts there so I said, 'Round them up because I have a packet of papers and two matches.' So we picked them all up, knocked the ash off, broke them up and we had enough for a smoke each.

Then Johnny turned up with his tin and it was a tin of rice of all things. I thought, 'Jesus, we'll eat this up tonight' as we had plenty of water, providing we could get the fire going. So I got to work and finally we had a fire going. With only two matches I couldn't take any chances.

We filled our bucket with water and were watching it heating up when all of a sudden we heard a noise. We looked up and at the top of the little escarpment there was an armoured car with its bloody guns trained down on us. I said to Pommy, 'What the hell are they?' and then we realised they were ours. They were Pommies.

We sang out and waved. Down the side of the escarpment there was something like a goat track and it led into the hollow. Anyway, down this track came this armoured car, then a second, and then a third one appeared on top with its guns pointed at us. The first car stopped about 50 metres away but kept its gun turret pointed directly at us.

I could see an officer standing in the turret so I called out, 'Thank Christ, you're the best sight we've seen,' and we heard him say, 'They're bloody Australians.' It turned out that they used to come in and water there every few days and they knew that Jerry also used it.

I asked 'Were you here this morning?' and they said 'No, not today.' I replied, 'Well Jerry was, there was still water in that tin, so we picked the right blokes.' The bloke in charge said, 'We'll get the hell out of here now. We don't want to get caught in here.' So they filled up their water tanks and one of us went to each car, and then we took off. The name of the well was 'Bir-Tengeddar'. I'll never forget it.

We got well away somewhere out in the desert and the sergeant said, 'We'll camp here for the night.' They split up and each car camped about a quarter of a mile apart as they would never group. It presented too large a target.

Anyway, these jokers said, 'Right, we're just about due to go back and we're short on rations but we've got some powdered eggs here' and that sounded like a banquet to us, so they cooked up these powdered eggs and we had army ration biscuits and had a great feed. But gee we were crook after, it bloody near killed us. Our stomachs were obviously in shocking condition.

It was the evening of 26 March and they had been in the desert for 11 days and had walked for about 225 km. They were made as comfortable as possible and had a good night's sleep for the first time since the crash.

The following day we headed back towards their advance base, and that consisted of only a few vehicles in a bit of a waddy. The next afternoon they told us that they had organised a ride for us back to their main base on three of their supply trucks the following afternoon.

On that day, just after lunch, we heard an aircraft approaching and next thing an old three-engined Italian Savoia came over the top of us. They must have been the biggest dopes in the world because they were flying at about 300 feet [90 m] and the whole crew were looking down at us. One of the sergeants in the armoured cars had replaced his standard issue Browning .303 with a Breda, an Italian gun and a damned good one; about a 50 calibre which packed a hell of a wallop.

As this bloody old thing circled at about 300 feet, almost over the top of us, the sergeant opened up with the Breda and I could see those slugs tearing into that aircraft, hitting at the wing root, and the next thing I could see fuel pouring out. The next minute she dived straight in. I often remember there were four blokes in that Savoia looking down on us, and three seconds later, they were all dead. Just as quick as that.

Our rescuers turned out to be a Long Range Desert Patrol from the Royal Dragoons and luckily for us they were prowling around behind Jerry lines. Anyway, their re-supply vehicles picked us up and we finally got back to our squadron. On the way back we rode one to each truck.

I was in the lead one and there were tracks going everywhere. My driver was scarping along and all of a sudden something sort of gelled so I said, 'Hang on a minute, pull up quick.' The driver said, 'What's up Sarge?' and I said 'You won't believe it but we're in the middle of a bloody minefield.' I stood on the running board and directed him back slowly, exactly in our tracks until we got back about 100 metres and onto hard stony ground.

Our luck was still holding. Jerry had laid thousands of mines throughout the Western Desert. Pommy and Johnny came up in their trucks and asked what was wrong. I said, 'Don't go down there, it's a bloody minefield.' It had made my hair stand on end.

When we got back to base all our gear had gone. We reckon the Pommie stores blokes had got hold of it and split it up between them. They were a mob of vultures. The Medical Officer gave us a check out and we had a bit of a blow out that night with our mob in the mess. We were told that we were going up to Cairo on a month's special sick leave and they had a vehicle which we could drive ourselves if we wanted to. The MO gave us a couple of letters to take to Cairo to make sure that we would be looked after. I was only in Cairo for about 4 days when I collapsed from Enteric Fever.

However we all got over it and as we were eventually away from the squadron for over six weeks, we were taken off Squadron strength and posted out to new squadrons. We were posted to 55 Squadron which was another English squadron.

That prang was on our very first raid. I had been in three earlier prangs while back in OUT [Operational Training Unit], so I said to Johnny one day, 'Jesus Johnny, we're not long for this world. The first one we do, we get whacked.' After I joined 55 squadron, I was on my sixth op when we got hit with Ack Ack and I was wounded in the right foot by shrapnel, so I was off strength again for about two months because the wound wouldn't heal.

While I was in Cairo again on sick leave I heard that Johnny and Pommy had got split up, and one day I bumped into some mates and they said, 'We've got bad news for you Mick,' so I said, 'What's up?'. They told me that Johnny had bought it. The CO of the squadron had wanted a gunner and he picked Johnny to go with him. They took a direct hit by a 88 mm shell, right on the bloody nose. They never knew what hit them.

I was then posted to 454 Squadron, which was a new all-Australian outfit forming up in Iraq. This squadron had Blenheims but was in the throes of changing over to

Martin Baltimores. That was where I ran into Paddy Archer again, my old pilot from OTU. He said 'Who are you flying with Mick?' and I said 'You,' and he said, 'That'll do me,' so we teamed up. I'd been there about four days when the adjutant approached us and said, 'I've got a job for you fellas, a holiday', so we were immediately very suspicious.

He told us that Ferry Command wanted a loan of an experienced crew to ferry an aircraft out to India, so that job took us a month. When we came back, we picked up with the squadron and went back to the Western Desert where we became fully operational again. It was a damn good squadron; they were all Australians. So that was that. I did another 12 months operational flying with Paddy on 454. When I tallied it up, Paddy and I did 87 operations together, for me a grand total of 93. It was a hell of a lot.

Back in Australia, my mother had received the following two telegrams from the Air Board.

"20 March 1942—Regret to inform you that your husband Sergeant Reginald Norman Ey is reported missing as result air operations in Middle East on 16th March 1942. Any further information received will be immediately conveyed to you. 12.40pm. Air Board."

"4 April 1942—Pleased to inform you that your husband Sergeant Reginald Norman Ey previously reported missing has been found safe and has returned to Unit. Your husband's aircraft made a forced landing in Libya on 16th March. He with other members of the crew travelled on foot until 26th March when they were picked up by a British patrol."

Pommy, Mick and Johnny (posthumously) were later made members of the Late Arrivals Club, membership of which was restricted to aircrew who had been forced down or crashed in the Western Desert and had taken longer than 48 hours to walk to the safety of their own lines. By war's end, there were only 80-odd members of this exclusive Air Force group. The badge depicts of a silver winged Flying Boot.

Supplied by Tony Ey of Queensland

47 DAYS IN A LEAKY BOAT

Wing Commander J R Jeudwine
84 Squadron Royal Air Force (including 30 Royal Australian Air Force personnel)
Java 1942

O ne of the most incredible escapes made during World War II involved 12 airmen who sailed in an open boat from Java [now Indonesia] to Australia to escape the Japanese, a journey that took 47 days. **The journey included being hit by violent tropical storms, becalmed on several occasions, having to constantly bail out a leaking boat, enduring visits from whales and sharks and an unlikely encounter with a Japanese submarine that let them pass unhindered.**

The 12 men from 84 Squadron RAF who made the journey were chosen for their stamina, morale and initiative. They were selected 'as it was felt they should be given a chance of reaching their home country', according to the log of the voyage written by Wing Commander J R Jeudwine.

They made their desperate escape bid after a surprise Japanese raid had captured their base, including about 20 Blenheim bombers and all support crew. After the Japanese attack, the aircrew had been sent from their base at Kalidjati near Bandoeng to the port of Tjilatjap for evacuation but the expected rescue ship never arrived to pick them up. They then decided to try and escape by sea and looked around for a suitable vessel.

All they could find were two old 9-metre lifeboats without engines. After an attempt to tow the heavily laden boats, each carrying about 30 men, out of the harbour ended in failure, and the wrecking of one lifeboat, it was decided the surviving boat, with a crew limited to 12 men, should try to reach Australia to get help for those left behind.

A search of the port area produced enough food and water for the 12 men to last about 30 days, twice as long as the anticipated 16-day duration of the journey, together with a large quantity of American canned beer that had been obtained from a Dutch canteen. Wing Commander Jeudwine made a note in his log of the voyage.

Painting of *Scorpion* by Athol Snook showing their daring escape.

This latter undoubtedly largely contributed to the well-being of the crew as the water had to be very strictly rationed and the beer was a food in itself.

The lifeboat was named *Scorpion* after the 84 Squadron badge and took the motto *Scorpiones ungent* (a scorpion stings).

They calculated that the nearest port on the Australian coast was Roeburns, 950 nautical miles (1530 km) away, with Port Headland and Onslow a little further away. They only had basic navigating equipment which included a marine sextant, a Mercator's Projection of the World, a portion of the Nautical Almanac giving declination tables and time apparent noon, a large scale chart of Java and Bali and a general navigation chart of the world (not discovered until after they reached Australia), but the men set off full of hope. There was no chronometer and they used the CO's watch, which was the only one working. They set off on 7 March 1942.

In view of these preparations, or lack of preparations, the following pages show the enormous luck which attended the *Scorpion* and her crew on the 47 days.

Those selected to take part in the epic voyage were Wing Commander J R Jeudwine (captain), Squadron Leader A K Passmore (2i/c and purser), Flying Officer C P L Streatfield (1st Lieutenant), Pilot Officer S G Turner (navigator)—all RAF—and Pilot Officer M S Macdonald, Sergeants G W Sayer, W N Cosgrove, A C Longmore, J Lovegrove, A C E Snook, P M Corney and P Haynes—all RAAF.

The first problem arose even before they left when they discovered an extra man on board, so he was sent ashore. Then strong winds prevented the boat from being rowed out of the cove and it had to be towed. Thunderstorms also caused some delay but once these had subsided, the oars came back out.

The following day the rudder came adrift, having been damaged in earlier manoeuvres, and had to be repaired. The crew was beginning to suffer from the cramped conditions and sunburn and, even when they made an awning to protect themselves, the heat was stifling.

On 9 March they had a narrow escape.

> No sooner had we got under way when a Japanese submarine bearing the marking 56 surfaced about a mile astern and steered towards us. She closed to within 100 yards [90 metres] and we were scrutinised through a pair of binoculars by an officer on the conning tower. One rating was standing by the 6pdr gun forward and another was manning a machine gun on the conning tower.

We expected to be shot at or captured but after describing a half circle round us, the submarine made off towards the east and eventually submerged. This was regarded as a lucky omen.

As soon as the submarine was sighted, each man was given a can of beer to drink in case they were killed or captured or the submarine turned out to be American—and therefore dry.

Later a heavy thunderstorm enabled them to replenish their water casks, which had leaked. The rain was so heavy that a 12 gallon [54 litre] cask was refilled in half an hour.

During the day, crew members took turns at swimming in the sea while the rest kept a look out for unwelcome visitors. Throughout the voyage they had several close encounters with sharks and a number of whales, so the lookouts always had to be vigilant.

Due to the basic nature of the navigation equipment and the unreliability of the only working watch, they were never sure exactly how far they had travelled, while the various currents and winds threatened on many occasions to take them away from their intended destination.

The rudder was a constant problem, regularly breaking away from the boat and having to be repaired. Great ingenuity was used to replace bits that had broken off in heavy seas.

Water rations were replenished whenever it rained and food stocks seemed to be holding out. But the original estimate of 16 days at sea was soon passed and rationing was tightened.

Lunch each day consisted of biscuits and two sardines or a little potted meat and a mouthful of water issued at noon.

From time to time the boat was becalmed while on other occasions storms hit them.

> Another foul night. Pouring rain and no wind. Whisky passed round to keep out the wet and cold and to enable us to sleep in spite of the discomfort.

During heavy seas the crew had to keep up constant bailing as the boat was in constant danger of becoming water logged. Steering was hampered by the lack of a reefing device on the sails and it was often difficult to keep the boat moving in the right direction.

After 24 days at sea, food stocks were found to be better than thought and allocations were increased but were reduced again after they were becalmed for several days. The boat was drifting northwards, away from Australia during these calm periods.

> A few more of these calms and we would be up the creek.

> During this calm we have rigged the awning after breakfast and organised games competitions between the quarter deck and the fo'c'sle. These have kept us occupied and helped pass the time but we found that the mental exercise made us very hungry and the talking and arguing brought on thirst. These are easier to bear than monotony.

Throughout the voyage, the men managed to maintain a sense of humour, although on 1 April, jokes were few and far between.

> The penalty for April Fools about ships or land was loss of beer ration for the rest of the voyage.

But some of the little things took on an importance much greater than normal. On 8 April Wing Commander Jeudwine wrote the following.

> Smoked last cigarette this evening. Had made a contract with four members of the crew to save their butts. These were carefully saved and kept in a tin. It meant I could have an occasional pipe. Will never again despise old men picking up fag ends from the gutter—I know just how they feel.

The next day they were visited by a young whale, which took a particular interest in them.

> Young whale, about 50–60 feet long [15–18 metres], surfaced about 200 yards [180 metres] away and decided to give us a close inspection. Eventually came to rest lying in a curve with its tail under the boat and poked its head out of the water certainly not more than three feet [1 metre] from the rudder.

> We could see the eye and mouth under water. We all hoped it would not become playful or try to make its toilet in the bottom of the boat, and luckily, after looking at us for about half a minute, which seemed like half an age, it submerged and went to join another whale which looks about four times as big.

> I hope the other one was its mother and she tore him off a strip for going and staring at strangers. When we had regained the power of movement we passed round a bottle of Australian 3 star brandy, which we had been keeping for an emergency, after which we did not care if we saw elephants, pink or otherwise, flying over us in tight formation.

On 16 April the crew had the first inkling that they might be nearing land.

> Sgt Corney swore he smelt spinifex on the dawn breeze. Soon he had everyone smelling something but personally put it down to the Purser who suffers from flatulence. However, everyone very cheerful. Plans for first meal ashore wildly discussed.

Wing Commander Jeudwine spent a sleepless night working out times of sunrise and sunset during the past few days then dropped a bombshell to the crew.

> The noon sight was due to my watch—the only one to survive—losing four minutes a day and that it might have lost as much as 40 minutes. This would have put us 600 miles west of Port Headland and about 250 miles west of the westernmost point of Australia.

> Rations, water and beer dramatically cut down and an accurate check shows that we can last for another six weeks on this new scale. We shall all be in pretty poor condition by the end of that time. Thank God the water will last that time, as it is one of the most important items, ranking equally with beer.

But early on 20 April they sighted land.

> It appeared to be a small island, and as the only island marked on our map was Barrow Island, which was quite a big piece of land, we reckoned this was a spit of the mainland and decided to carry on until we could make certain.

Soon, they set foot on dry land for the first time in 45 days.

> All members of crew very weak but looked forward to a hot breakfast. Food issued ad lib and cocoa made, but people found that they could not eat as much as they thought, with the exception of the First Lieutenant who proved a fine trencherman. Purser feeling sick, probably reaction but might be the sight of so much food being issued at one meal.

They continued their voyage after breakfast and sighted an unidentified aircraft high and about 16 km to the west of them. Their efforts to attract its attention failed and they landed on another small island for the night, enjoying a stable, soft bed made from spinifex.

Next day they spotted a flying boat, which turned out to be a Catalina of Patrol Squadron 101, US Navy. Waving all manner of clothing, they eventually persuaded the Catalina to land but the crew of the aircraft were still suspicious and kept their weapons handy.

After exchange of signals, of a sort, I swam over to flying boat, beating all existing records for ocean swimming in my anxiety to dodge any sharks that night be around. Was given a rope to hang on to but in spite of the fact that I was mother naked except for my beard I was menaced by a man with a Colt .45 who would not let me on board until he was quite satisfied that I was harmless. Maybe he was right but someone should have told him about sharks.

The captain of the aircraft offered to take six of the crew from the boat but only three accepted the offer—the others opted to stay with the boat. However, the next day another Catalina landed and picked up the rest of the crew and the boat was abandoned.

So, after 47 days, having sailed approximately 1500 statute miles, leaking like a sieve but still serviceable, with a jury rudder fitted from the second day out, *Scorpion* was cast adrift off the NW coast of Australia without the honour of being sailed into port.

Thus ended an epic voyage under incredible conditions that enabled 12 men to escape the clutches of the Japanese. Those left behind in Java were all taken prisoner and most worked on the Burma–Thailand railway where many died.

Supplied by Gwen Atkinson of Western Australia

Wing Commander Jeudwine attempting to board the US Navy Catalina.
Sketch by Athol Snook.

'ONE THING MORE–GOODBYE'

Flying Officer Athol Snook
100 Squadron, Royal Australian Air Force
New Guinea 1942

F lying Officer Athol Snook was a survivor. He was one of the 12 airmen from 84 Squadron RAAF who endured 47 days at sea in a lifeboat sailing from Java to Australia to escape from the Japanese. Then he was posted to the newly formed 100 Squadron RAAF and, on a fateful night in New Guinea later that year, his Beaufort bomber was grounded while the rest of the squadron went to attack Japanese shipping. Three aircraft failed to make it back.

Some years later, Athol Snook wrote an article in remembrance of his mates in New Guinea. His memory was triggered by a chance conversation about a radio program that was popular during the war. Many programs of their day featured certain catch phrases that always brought roars of laughter from the audience. Athol Snook takes up the story.

Funny thing how memory works. A scent, an old tune or sometimes a taste can start your mind throwing up pictures that you thought you'd forgotten forever.

I don't suppose there are many people today who remember Harry Tate and his wonderful radio sketch 'Running an Office' all about Tootles the office boy, the mad inventor and the mousetrap.

Well, the other night I heard Harry Tate's name mentioned at a party. We were all very much of an age, somewhere in our 50s—what might be called 'older boys and girls'. That's if one were being kind that is. Standing there in a mild alcoholic haze, well fed and at peace with the world, I was suddenly whisked out of that lounge, plucked from my friends and transported over the Indian Ocean, across the shallow Timor Sea, through the Torres Straits and straight into Milne Bay at the most eastern tip of New Guinea. Not only was this instantaneous, or nearly so, but there was a neat

---

Self-portrait of Athol Snook.

little bit of time wangling as well. Without any fuss or nonsense the clock was turned back and suddenly it was 1942.

If you look at a map of New Guinea you'll notice that there's something about its shape that reminds you of some crouching primitive animal. What used to be called Dutch New Guinea is the head with gaping mouth; at the other end, with forked tail, is where we were. Between these two points is the almost virgin world of this huge island. Dramatic, mountainous, jungle covered. Dangerous. Peopled by ochre-painted, sometimes warlike natives. A land where salt is a form of currency and where the plumes of the Bird of Paradise crown heads with exotic beauty.

This was the last link in the chain of island conquests which the Japanese had to secure before they turned south for the greatest prize of all—Australia.

That they never achieved their goal can only be called a miracle. They were beaten in the Battle of the Coral Sea and on land were stopped when only a handful of miles from Moresby. The battles along the Kokoda Trail were bitter, bloody and heroic.

Milne Bay was the end of the line for the Japs; they were beaten there too and withdrew and that's how our squadron came to be stationed there. We flew Beaufort torpedo bombers, operated from a strip cut out of a coconut plantation and lived in a village of brown-coloured tents. Mud, sweat, mildew, rain and the thud of falling coconuts were the elements of our domestic life. Mosquitoes enlivened the nights with their whining flight and now and again the Japs brightened things up with their unwelcome and noisy visits. It is against this backdrop that the scene is played.

Don Leigh, a gunner, was little, untidy and wore badly fitting false teeth. He nearly always sported a filthy, battered topee and his shorts were too long. In civilian life he had been a radio announcer in Hobart. He had a wonderful, wicked sense of humour. I thought he was the funniest thing since Charlie Chaplin.

Bill Young was just the opposite. Good looking, pipe smoking, he exuded an atmosphere of calm control. He even managed to look clean. Both he and I were navigators. All of us treasured a battered portable gramophone; our greatest joy was to play a very noisy and scratchy recording of Colonel Corn. Vera Lynn brought emotional lumps to our throats and we wallowed in colourful and no doubt erotic memories of life 'down south'. Harry Tate, with his 'Running an Office' sketch was the perfect 'middle of the road' distraction. It neither enraged our neighbours nor reduced us to emotional wrecks.

There were endless ways of introducing catch phrases from the sketch into the general conversation and it became a sort of bond to our friendship, rather like belonging to a secret society which has some form of ritual known only to the initiated. Others not in the know would be puzzled by odd references to 'being back in the spring' or that we were 'closing the office'. The favourite, however, was to call someone back who was already some distance off and say, in a hesitating and vague way 'Oh—eh—one thing more—goodbye'. This had the satisfying effect of infuriating the victim. It was the last line of the sketch and we used it whenever possible. Childish? Perhaps; but it was a form of escape from the monotony and yes, the fears of those days so long ago.

We were down at the strip when news came in that there was a Japanese naval force consisting of a cruiser and destroyers within striking distance of our planes. No one who has not experienced the chill which strikes when you know that you are going to risk your neck within the next few hours can imagine fully how it feels. Nine crews were put on immediate stand by. Aircraft were to be checked. Take-off was to be just before dusk. It started to rain. A depressing half light did nothing to brighten the atmosphere.

Then our machine went U/S [unserviceable] with hydraulic trouble and we as a crew were withdrawn from the strike; we went to the briefing just the same, relieved to be out of what looked like being a very sticky 'do', yet carried along by the impetus of our near involvement.

The Ops Room was a thatched hut, trestle tables end-to-end split the room in half down its length. Wall maps of the area showed the military situation. The enemy ships' position was almost due east of the bay. The room was crowded, it smelt of dampness, sweat and cigarette smoke. The hard light of pressure lamps seemed to intensify the late afternoon gloom. It was to be a classic torpedo attack with the planes coming in at the cruiser from three different directions. It was simple enough—fly out in formation, find the enemy in the half dark, split up, attack and destroy. Then come home independently. All one had to do was to do it.

The briefing came to an end. The crews collected their belongings, nav. bags, headphones, survival kits. All the paraphernalia of bomber crews. Gradually the room cleared. My two friends moved towards the door; I stood watching. As if suddenly remembering something, Don turned. He came a few steps towards me and with a little smile said 'Oh—one thing more—goodbye.'

One by one the planes racketed into life, taxied to the take-off point. Propellers hurled the streaming air behind and wheels crashed over the shining metal matting. They lifted into the weeping dusk heading towards the east. The sound of their motors faded and we were left with only the hissing of the lamp and the dripping rain.

And so we waited, making conversation for the sake of appearing normal but our minds carried us out over a grey sea that swept so close beneath our wings and suddenly there they are; dark smudges wildly swinging in an agony of evasion. Split up—line astern. Now the leading plane banks, turning in towards the ship. Now line abreast. Steady at 120 knots and 120 feet. Not much to remember, just do it. Now the grey shapes show little flicks of light along their sides. What's that? They're firing at us, that's all. Get in close. Now the great shape seems to fill the windshield. Now is the moment. Bomb doors open. Press the tit. A slight jolt and the torpedo slices away from the plane. It is done, now nothing can change what is going to happen. The planes swerve and jink. The navigators spray madly with their twin Vickers. The pilots sweat with an agony of tension as they battle to avoid the other planes and now they are pulling back on the control column and the great ship is whipping beneath. Planes seem to be everywhere. The ships fire madly. Skidding and weaving the aircraft climb away. The cruiser explodes in a thundering, tearing spasm of tortured metal, inrushing sea and screeching steam. It is all over. The planes turn towards the west and home. Now it is almost night and the rain beats against the wings.

We sat in the tent waiting. Overhead the palms move their fronds restlessly like great living, questing hairy creatures, dark against the weeping night. Now the sound of engines filling the dripping sky with the sad, lonely throb of their beat. One by one they come in to land, their brilliant lights seeking the sodden strip. Great dark shapes moving against a hedge of palms. The tyres touch, kissing the metal, sobbing in a watery embrace. Four down, four more to come. Now once more the sound, the piercing light the mad careering shape—it goes on and on throwing up great gobs of water, it cannot stop in time. The pilot pulls up the undercart, the plane slithers obscenely in the mud like some poor broken bird. Rescue teams rush to help but there is no need, there is no fire and the crew climb out unhurt.

Once more we wait and now the fear for our friends grows stronger, feeding on doubt, it spreads among the group of men who stand out in the rain straining their ears for the beat of propellers. The weather worsens, the palms bend to the rising wind. Squalls of rain lash obliquely at the planes, the flapping tents, the dripping jungle. Sheet lightning lights the world around like a series of false dawns, thunder rumbles, truculent, threatening. Suddenly we hear the plane. At first it is only a whisper, but quickly the sound grows stronger, as if gaining confidence. Now it is overhead drowning the other sounds with its pulsing beat. We can even see the navigation lights, red and green twin wandering stars, misted by the rain, sweeping in concentric orbits till they are lost to sight in the pounding rain. Again and again the scene is repeated. The plane is very low, circling and circling. Over the E/T the voice of the radio operator strained but controlled, his message, broken by static, tells the story. Visibility is so bad that they cannot see the strip lights well enough to attempt a landing. Fuel is getting very low.

The CO makes the decision. They must gain height, set the machine on a course for the bay and bale out. It is the best chance they have.

Now the engine note becomes stronger, more purposeful. They pass over us once more and the sound of their flight echoes from the crouching hills as they head for the sea. Suddenly, there is the dull boom of an explosion, then silence, only the wind and rain.

The jungled arms of the bay have caught them in a wet embrace; the swaying trees and tangled vines ripped and torn by the violence of the union; the black wet earth laid bare by their metal plough. A self dug grave for four young men. Ken Magregor, pilot, Bill Young, navigator, Frank Ewing, radio operator and Don Leigh, gunner.

Over the years I have often thought of them and of the other two crews who were lost that night, lost in the awful blind, wandering till they too found some mountain peak or watery end. I can still see the hissing lamp, still smell the musty jungle damp, still see the little figure with the battered topee, the long shorts and from the past a ghostly, taunting voice calls me back, intoning 'One thing more—goodbye.'

Supplied by Gwen Atkinson of Western Australia

HUGGING THE GROUND
IN NEW GUINEA

Leading Aircraftman Elton 'Tony' Booth
100 Squadron, Royal Australian Air Force
New Guinea 1943–1944

Being shot at by planes and having bombs dropped near you was a fairly common occurrence in New Guinea during World War II, as Tony Booth would be the first to tell you. But when the bullets and the bombs came from Australian aircraft, it was a bit hard to take.

Tony Booth was an aircraft mechanic, a job which had its dangerous moments, especially when guns were fired accidentally while the planes were being serviced or when bombs were dropped as they were being mounted under the wings of the Beaufort bombers.

Tony was at Milne Bay in New Guinea with 100 Squadron RAAF when he received his 'own' aircraft to look after. He later wrote about this experience in *The Dry Gullies I Have Crossed*.

> A plane would be allocated generally to two men, a mechanic and a rigger, but quite often only to a mechanic.
>
> It was then your responsibility to see it was in 100% order at all times and the aim of the serviceability was to ensure that as many as possible would be available in the shortest possible time.
>
> First thing every morning we would do our daily inspection, which was a very thorough visual inspection to see nothing was broken or displaced. We would then 'pull the motor through' which involved turning the airscrews (propellers) over a few times, draining the petrol tanks via the drain cocks under each tank, letting the petrol run into your hand to see if any water had got in from overnight condensation.

Tony Booth (right) with mate and Beaufort, Goodenough Island, 1944.

We did 40-hourly and 80-hourly inspections on the aircraft and if an inspection was due on an aircraft it would be taken to an inspection bay which had a camouflage net stretched over it. This was our workshop in the open.

It was during one of these inspections that Tony had a scare.

I was working on an engine on an 80-hourly inspection and just beside me was Neil Phelan, taking an oil cooler out of the leading edge of a mainplane (wing).

All of a sudden two machine-guns (one in each wing) let go a burst of fire. I froze for a few seconds and so did Neil as he was closer to the gun than I was. It appears that a rigger was up in the cockpit and pressed the firing button on the pilot's joy stick and it was not on 'safe', or so the man said.

Tony endured another thrilling few minutes one day at Milne Bay. He was working on his aircraft and in the dispersal bay opposite a new armourer who was being shown over a Beaufort and getting some practice.

The next moment I heard 'Clatter! Clatter!' and looked out of the corner of my eye to see the last of the bombs hitting the metal stripping across the road. I instinctively 'hugged the ground', as we used to term a quick fall to the ground in an emergency. I did not have time to feel how my heart pounded. I just listened and, of course, nothing happened.

The armourer had apparently told the new armourer never to press the jettison button but, as he did so, he mechanically pressed the button and the bombs had fallen out of their mountings. They had not exploded because, even though they were fused, they had fallen on their side and had not landed on their point to activate the detonator.

I know I knew this at the time but you never take risks and in the few feet the bombs had to fall, they were kept safe and fell onto their sides. Some time later I was in the vicinity when another wing bomb fell to the ground accidentally and it remained intact also.

During the wet season it was not unusual for aircraft to get bogged.

A couple of times we got hauled out of bed at sunrise to get a plane out of a bog. It was too wet to get a tractor in so what we would do was to get as many 'bodies' as possible to get a purchase on the plane and to push.

The pilot would start up and 'gun' the engines and we would push. We had the slip-stream to push against as well as an unsure footing underneath and a bit of flying soft mud, but we would get them out onto firmer ground.

Pat Cannon, Bob Smith and Arthur Innocenzi with 250 lb and 500 lb bombs.

One night Tony was woken by a loud crash, followed by a burst of ack-ack fire.

> We could not make it out at this time in the morning but at breakfast we found out all about it. Our planes had gone out on a 'bash' and a Japanese aircraft followed the last one in to avoid being detected by radar. It let some bombs drop and had got one aircraft in its dispersal bay just as it taxied in and the anti-aircraft fire was more or less a token shot in the dark.

The ground staff duty crew were lucky that night. It was part of their duty to be at the dispersal bay to check the crew and plane on parking but their truck had broken down and they were delayed in getting there.

When they finally arrived, they found the pilot sitting in front of the Beaufort in a dazed condition, one of the crew lying near the aircraft with shrapnel in his leg and another taking a 'nervous leak'. The observer was found to be dead when they opened the underneath hatch to look for him.

> I had a particular interest in this plane as it was 'mine' and it presented quite a desolate sight next morning. The bomb was a daisy-cutter that landed alongside the plane, puncturing all the tyres, rupturing the oil tank, and even though there was oil everywhere, there was no fire and the self-sealing petrol tanks did their job to perfection.

On another occasion, Tony completed an aircraft inspection and went on the inspection flight with the crew.

> We took off and after a while I looked out the side and saw the starboard airscrew was in the fully feathered position. This was normally done only in case of emergency. It made the airscrew parallel to the plane and the air going past it would not let it turn and would thus stop any further damage to an engine. I nearly collapsed when I saw it and the WAG [Wireless/Air Gunner] in the crew saw my apprehension when I thought 'What has gone wrong in the inspection?' It was something every mechanic dreaded, on his plane at any rate.

He was given a big thumbs-up so he was reassured that all was in order, but he became concerned again later when the pilot banked sharply, flew over the airstrip and 'shot it up', then came in and landed, all on one engine.

> When we landed and parked in our bay the pilot said there was nothing wrong with the plane.

He learned later that the pilot had been showing off how reliable a Beaufort was even on one engine. After another pilot had pulled a similar stunt, the commanding officer called a halt to the business because of the danger to crews and ground staff.

Tony had another narrow escape when bullets from a Kittyhawk of 75 Squadron came flying through the air. The aircraft was having its guns synchronised, so the bullets crossed at a certain distance in front of it, when the electric firing mechanism jammed. It did not stop firing until both magazines were empty.

> We were pleased to hear the silence again but it was a bit frightening to see tracer bullets as momentarily you see them at a distance before you hear the guns. I did not think it was the best place to be with bullets flying past at only chest height and once more sought refuge on the ground till the firing finished.

After some home leave Tony took another course to become an engine fitter and this brought a rise in pay. He was posted to Rathmines working on Catalinas and then on to C-47s (commonly known as DC-3s) taking supplies up to New Guinea.

> This part of my service was a breeze, especially after my previous time 'up there' of nearly 15 months.

Supplied by Elton 'Tony' Booth of Queensland

THE ACCIDENTAL COASTWATCHER

Sub-Lieutenant Frederick Ashton 'Snow' Rhoades US DSC & Silver Star
Coastwatcher, Royal Australian Naval Volunteer Reserve
Solomon Islands 1942–1945

C oastwatchers in the Pacific played an important role in the Allied victory in World War II. They defied the odds and constant danger of being caught by the Japanese to feed vital information to the Allies.

Many of the coastwatchers fell into the role by accident. Frederick Ashton 'Snow' Rhoades was manager of Burns Philp's copra and rubber Lavaro Plantation on the north-west coast of Guadalcanal in 1942.

When the British Solomon Islands Protectorate (BSIP) capital Tulagi was attacked by the Japanese, the Solomon Islands were evacuated, but Snow decided to stay put and become a coastwatcher.

He was no stranger to danger, having ridden with the 1st Light Horse Regiment, Australian Imperial Force, in the Middle East during World War I. A boy from the bush, Snow was an expert horseman and a crack shot—an ideal candidate for the Light Horse.

He was twice wounded in action and suffered constantly from malaria, but took part in the long campaign from the Sinai Desert to Jordan. After the war he spent some time as a jackeroo and seven years as a soldier settler near Inverell, NSW, before walking off the property in the middle of the Depression.

It was then he joined Levers Pacific Plantations in the Solomon Islands as a plantation overseer. He soon made a mark for himself and was promoted to manager three years later. He became very popular with the local people, taking them hunting, using his marksman skills to kill wild cattle and distributing much of the fresh meat among the locals. He also formed cricket teams from the locals and organised regular matches.

Sub-Lieutenant Snow Rhoades

So, when he decided to stay after the evacuation, he had a solid support base among the local population. His initial plan of defending his plantation against the Japanese was abandoned when he realised that his small native force was no match for the well-armed and trained Japanese.

He acquired a 3BZ AWA short-wave radio and, knowing there was no way he could leave the island until it was recaptured by the Allies, he began his new role in life. The one down side to the operation was that as a civilian, he would certainly have been shot if captured. He was offered the position of unpaid sergeant in the BSIP Defence Force but declined. In April 1942 he was made a sub-lieutenant in the Royal Australian Naval Volunteer Reserve (RANVR).

Commander Eric Feldt, the coastwatchers' commanding officer, made it very clear that their mission was to observe and report enemy activity, stay alive and only fight in self-defence. Their reports on enemy movements and losses were a lot more important to the Allied cause than the deaths of a few Japanese soldiers.

The Japanese were very active in the area and Snow, with a fellow coastwatcher, Leif Schroeder, a Norwegian, would call up US air strikes on the ships and barges operating in the area.

On one occasion, Snow was returning by motor launch from a trip to nearby islands when they were spotted by a Japanese aircraft. As dawn approached they saw a Japanese destroyer heading for them. They quickly disappeared through an opening in the reef and the destroyer headed back out to sea. On their next broadcast they reported its presence and the ship was attacked and sunk by US aircraft.

Expecting enemy patrols to find their bungalow at any time, Snow prepared a number of safe houses at strategic intervals in the bush. The radio equipment was big and heavy and required about 20 carriers to move it from place to place, so they needed early warning for any move.

Snow gave up wearing shoes so his footprints would not give the game away. He decided to burn his plantation buildings, including all the rubber in store, and move away from the coast to the Hylovo River where he could count on the support of Chief Pellissi.

The Japanese were now seriously tracking broadcasts using flying boats fitted with direction finding equipment and had placed a bounty of £100 on Snow's head, a huge attraction for the local people.

Meanwhile, the Japanese began constructing a huge airfield on a grassy plain that was part of Lunga Plantation. The coastwatchers were in an ideal position to report on all activities and later, on aircraft movements.

But some of the local people believed that the Allies were losing the war, and were prepared to kill the coastwatchers and claim the reward. Chief Pellissi talked them out of carrying out their threat.

He also advised Snow to move his hide-out to a more secure cave. By now, food was running low and both Snow and Schroeder were having health problems, the constant stress having made them exhausted and quite ill.

In August 1942, the Americans realised that the enemy airfield at Lunga was ready for use and decided to capture it. In a surprise attack, which included HMAS *Canberra*, the area was heavily bombarded from the sea and the US 1st Marine Division landed at Tulagi and Lunga Point.

They captured the airfield with little resistance from the Japanese, most of the personnel on the site being construction corps workers. The taking of Lunga, however, did not improve the position of Snow and Schroeder, because the Japanese were now spread out further along the coast, making it harder for the coastwatchers to move around.

Reports came through of atrocities carried out by Japanese soldiers, including the murder of two priests and two nuns. Snow and his helpers kept track of Japanese movements and called in air strikes that disposed of many Japanese.

At the same time, the Allies didn't have it all their own way, with three US cruisers and HMAS *Canberra* all sunk in a surprise Japanese Navy night attack. The airfield, renamed Henderson, was under heavy attack from Japanese aircraft and casualties and aircraft losses were mounting.

It was becoming harder and harder for Snow and Schroeder to operate. Finally a request was made to US Marines commander General Vandegrift to get them out. He refused to help and forbade the senior coastwatcher, Lieutenant-Commander Hugh Mackenzie, from mounting a rescue mission.

Mackenzie decided to disobey the order and sent Sub-Lieutenant Dick Horton and a crew in a borrowed government schooner, *Ramada*, to pick them up. They successfully ran the gauntlet of enemy shipping during the night and collected Snow, Schroeder, 13 missionaries and a shot-down airman, as well as Snow's radio equipment.

After eight months dodging the Japanese, Snow spent some time at the receiving end of a bombardment by Japanese heavy bombers and then by the Japanese Navy that destroyed most of the Marine aircraft on the ground at Henderson.

Snow Rhoades and Edna Norman.

The arrival of a US fleet of light cruisers (8-inch guns) and destroyers, under the command of Rear Admiral Daniel Callaghan, brought relief to Henderson Field, after they defeated a much larger force of Japanese Navy ships, including two Kongo Class (14-inch guns) battleships. The gallant Callaghan was killed in this almost suicidal attack.

Snow Rhoades then returned to Australia where he had a month's leave and a month's sick leave, during which he married his long-time friend, Edna Norman. He also learned he had been awarded the US Distinguished Service Cross, the highest decoration that could be conferred on a foreigner by the US Forces, for his services as a coastwatcher.

But his role was not yet ended. He insisted on returning to Lunga in March 1943 and played an integral part in the successful capture of Rendova. His intimate knowledge of the area, where he had been a plantation manager, was invaluable in the operation.

In the next few weeks, Snow was involved in many small actions while patrolling the Rendova perimeter or hunting down parties of escaping Japanese. For gallantry in action during the Rendova operation, Snow was awarded the US Silver Star.

In 1946, Snow and Edna took up residence in Rabaul where he became a plantation inspector for three years. Then, in 1950, he was requested to return to the Navy with the rank of Lieutenant-Commander to reorganise the coastwatcher organisation in New Guinea and the Solomon Islands, a position he held until 1954.

He returned to New Guinea as Senior Produce Inspector for the Territory of Papua and New Guinea. At the age of 60, while still working full-time, he commenced planting a cocoa plantation and after retiring officially when he was 72, ran the plantation until 1973, when he sold up and moved to the Sunshine Coast in Queensland.

Supplied by Ted Rhoades of New South Wales

NO WALTZING AFTER
MATILDA HIT MINE

Corporal Des Lloyd
C Squadron, 1st Army Tank Battalion (AIF)
New Guinea 1943

Fighting in New Guinea was plagued by all sorts of problems, not the least being the terrain over which the troops had to travel. Heavy rain often turned tracks into quagmires and made progress hazardous to say the least.

Tanks, in particular, had difficulties navigating the jungle-clad, muddy hilly areas and this, combined with cunningly hidden Japanese minefields, caused a number of vehicles to come to grief.

The picture opposite shows 'Calamity Jane', a Matilda infantry support tank of C Squadron, 1st Army Tank Battalion (AIF) which had ground to a halt when it hit mines and lost a track during the drive north of Finschhafen.

The tank's crew included Lieutenant Sam Johnson (commander), Corporal Des Lloyd (gunner) and Trooper J Bramston (driver).

> It took a great deal of hard work to dig the damaged track out of the mud. We then had to repair and replace the track.

But just as they started up and moved off, they hit other mines that were lying undetected under the tank. It was by now a write-off, but luckily no-one was hurt in the explosion.

Supplied by Des Lloyd of New South Wales

Members of C Squadron, 1st Army Tank Battalion, repairing a Matilda tank in New Guinea.

'DEVOTION TO DUTY WORTHY OF THE HIGHEST PRAISE'

Flying Officer Ray Graetz
100 Squadron, Royal Australian Air Force
New Guinea 1944

F **lying Officer Ray Graetz was a wireless operator/air gunner on a bombing and strafing mission with eight other Beauforts over Wewak in May 1944 when his aircraft was shot down by enemy gunfire**

The pilot, Flying Officer Lyle McLaren, turned the Beaufort towards the sea, hoping to ditch it well away from land, but the cockpit rapidly filled with smoke and he was forced to ditch close to the shore, just 20 metres from the But Plantation and a strong force of Japanese troops.

> The dingy was released and we all climbed aboard it on the seaward side of the aeroplane. I re-entered the wireless compartment of the Beaufort to take care of the destruction of the classified equipment.

> Then we commenced to paddle the dinghy seaward but as we drew away from the shelter of the Beaufort lying in the surf, the Japanese opened up with several machine guns from the rising ground beyond But Mission.

The first burst killed the navigator, Flying Officer Sydney Anderson; the second holed the dingy, which immediately filled with water; and the third burst killed Flying Officer McLaren, completely collapsed the dingy and shot off the lobe of Ray Graetz's right ear.

> Catalina Sea Rescue had been contacted by accompanying aircraft. A Catalina had arrived and circled above us for quite a considerable time, but was unable to effect a rescue because of intense enemy fire from the shore.

Although not a strong swimmer, Ray Graetz headed westward along the coast while the only other survivor, Flight Sergeant Francis Maloney, swam seaward to escape the machine-gun fire.

Ray Graetz escaping from the ditched Beaufort.

My flying boots soon came off and were lost, as was the jungle kit that had gone down with the plane. I started swimming and drifting westward with the current about 200 yards [183 m] off shore.

The Japanese were still firing spasmodically and sent patrols along the beach but some distance back from the water's edge. Because of this they probably could not see me behind the waves.

Ray Graetz finally scrambled ashore where a solitary Japanese soldier apparently didn't see him as he crawled into the scrub. Feeling weak from the loss of blood caused by the wound to his ear, he crawled under a bush and just lay there, eventually falling asleep.

All Allied airmen had been warned about the dangers they faced if shot down and captured by the Japanese. 'Tokyo Rose', the Japanese propaganda broadcaster, had repeatedly warned that any airmen captured would have the muscles in their legs cut so they could not walk and would be left to die a slow and horrible death in the jungle.

It was with this thought in mind that Ray Graetz began an extraordinary eight-day episode during which he survived numerous encounters with Japanese troops, went without food for over a week, but still managed to sabotage various Japanese weapons and trucks.

He awoke about 10 pm that same evening and heard considerable motor truck activity going both ways along the coastal road. He tried to get a look at it but was so weak from loss of blood that he collapsed and just lay there till dawn.

I spent a wretched night being quite naked having lost my shirt and trousers crawling through the scrub. Awakening at dawn, I had enough strength to crawl back and locate my clothing, which was close by.

I felt very weak as my wound had bled through the night. Later, I became semi-delirious and so lay under a nearby bush for the rest of the day. I also slept there at night.

The next morning he decided to try to make his way to Tadji. At Au Creek, he found two bomb craters partially filled with clear water.

Having had nothing to drink yet, except dew from the leaves of bushes, I lay in a crater in the water for several hours drinking constantly. My total immersion in this crater probably saved my life. The absorption of fluid apparently counteracted the shock and loss of blood. When I eventually scrambled out of the crater, I was feeling totally fit again.

In the afternoon he made his way to But Drome where the runway was full of bomb craters and damaged Japanese aircraft.

He decided to travel at night and set off westward but at the mouth of Manil Creek he almost walked into a sentry who was sitting down looking out to sea. Soon afterwards, a party of 40 or so Japanese soldiers carrying lanterns arrived and started unloading trucks.

He lay watching this activity for 45 minutes or so and then crawled back to the beach and slept under another bush. He had had no food all day and felt very hungry.

The next morning he tried to build a raft from empty drums and coconut logs, but it collapsed on launching. He found some yellow phone lines that the Japanese had laid and cut 200 metres off them to tie the drums together, but this effort proved to be unsuccessful too.

Soon afterwards, several truckloads of troops arrived to investigate the interruption to their phone line.

> I lay under a bush and covered myself with kunai grass while they searched the area. One soldier actually stepped over my legs without seeing me, his sword was dangling by his side.

> Later, while walking along the beach, I located a camouflaged 3-inch gun on wheels pointing seaward in an open-back emplacement. I put several handfuls of sand down the muzzle and in the breech mechanism. Nearby were several weapon pits designed for machine guns.

> Spent the afternoon wandering around the But strip inspecting enemy planes. Found a waterproof sheet and the silk from a parafrag bomb there. Henceforth used the silk at night to wrap myself in so that my wet clothes would dry.

That evening, he spread grass on the leading edge of the mainplane of a Japanese aircraft and slept under it.

> At 6 am two Japanese came walking past the plane but did not see me as the grass provided shelter. They were each carrying a machine gun and had probably come from the weapons pits seen the previous afternoon.

Ray Graetz continued his journey and came across some huts where Japanese troops had been living. A strafing attack had recently been carried out so the dwellings had been abandoned.

> Entering the huts I took a water bottle and towels as well as some shirts. I went through the personal kit of someone but found nothing of interest.

> Just opposite the hut, a three-ton truck was pulled under the trees. It seemed serviceable so I pulled out the distributor wires.

He came across another group of huts that had been used as a dump for medical supplies. These were scattered about everywhere, apparently by a bomb blast. Continuing along, he saw six fuel tankers and an equal number of three-ton trucks.

Just as I pulled out the wiring from the distributors of two of the trucks, I saw two Japanese cross the track. They didn't see me.

Shortly afterwards he was caught in strafing by numerous Douglas A-20 Havocs (or Bostons) of the US Army Air Forces.

Taking shelter under a wide spreading tree just off the road, I found the experience terrifying as bombs exploded nearby and later a belly tank was dropped on the tree and hit by tracers.

The resultant fire burned part of the tree and half an acre of grass. Unfortunately, there were no enemy stores in that area.

He lay under a tree for the rest of the day and watched as 50 or so fully equipped troops began to assemble nearby.

Seven trucks came along and picked them up then headed in different directions. In view of the activity I slept under a large tree, sharing it with two Japanese who retired for the night on the opposite side. Waking the next morning, I found my companions had already gone.

During the morning he ran into at least six individual Japanese soldiers walking along the track.

They seemed to be very weary and I avoided them by stepping into the undergrowth.

He was starting to cross a creek when he spotted an elderly Japanese man crossing towards him.

I walked straight past and he took no notice. Just across the creek, in a clearing, I saw six armed soldiers. I walked right on past them. They merely looked and said nothing.

Several more were met, all walking eastward along the track. Some grunted as we passed so I grunted back a reply.

He still had not had any food but found he was losing the desire to eat, although he kept drinking from his water bottle.

Further on in a clearing he came across 20 soldiers resting with arms stacked.

All appeared to be smarter than others I had seen but they did nothing but sit up as I walked past. That night I slept well on the beach at Bai as I was now feeling stronger.

The next day he ignored the shouts of Japanese soldiers working on a bridge and they resumed their work when he made no reply.

Taking a course parallel to the coast through the thick scrub in the foothills, I came across a soldier boiling six billies of tea. He came towards me calling out but I waved my hand across my face as if in pain and walked on. I reached the Anumb River and found 100 troops bathing, whilst further downstream more were swimming and washing clothes.

Towards dusk, at the top of a high feature, I found a large log. As heavy rain had started I slept under it with leaves laid on each side to keep the rain out. I had lost the desire for food but consumed considerable water during the day.

He spent the following day battling through the thick bush in an effort to reach the coast again and he spent the night under yet another bush. The day after, he continued along a narrow track that he thought was probably invisible from the air as the undergrowth was both heavy and tall. He met several individual Japanese soldiers who were all too tired to take any notice of him.

Pushed on and finally reached the Danmap River. Whilst trying to cross, P-39s (US Airacobra fighters) flew over me from the west. Later, two came back and circled low down and waggled their wings. Still having the same small parachute, I waved in reply.

I waited until late afternoon thinking that perhaps a Catalina would arrive. I was surprised when two PT boats turned up and came towards me.

Just as a raft was lowered overboard to float ashore, Japanese soldiers opened fire on the boats.

The boats silenced the fire after a heavy strafing of the beach and village areas. They then returned and shot two lines to me but I was too weak to risk being carried away by a strong cross current so I did not retrieve the lines. Eventually two of the crewmen swam ashore with the raft and brought me to their vessel.

Ray Graetz was rescued by US patrol boats PT-128 and PT-131. Lieutenant William Stewart and Ensign Gregory Azarigian risked their lives by disregarding sniper fire to swim in and snatch him to safety.

The day after the medico on the mother boat had attended to him, Flying Officer Graetz was returned to his RAAF base at Nadzab, where he was interviewed.

I was able to pinpoint where I had seen supplies being unloaded from a Japanese submarine and was able to identify the location of groups of Japanese on river tributaries, where they sheltered under the overhanging jungle from Allied aircraft.

This detailed information of every moment of my time in the area was invaluable to the Army for the tactical planning of their assault on the Japanese-held area.

Flying Officer Graetz was later awarded the Military Cross for his 'outstanding courage, initiative and complete disregard for his own safety. His devotion to duty is worthy of the highest praise.'

Supplied by Ray Graetz of New South Wales

'THE ARMY AHEAD
OF THE ARMY'

Mr Jack McAulay
Civilian
Civilian Constructional Corps
Australia 1940–1945

While we are familiar with the efforts of the many young men who left Australia to fight overseas during World War II, we are less aware of one large group of men who made a significant contribution to the war effort back home.

These were the men of the Civil Constructional Corps (CCC) who were responsible for building many major facilities throughout Australia during World War II. The CCC was established in the dark days of the Pacific War and called for the skills of thousands of tradesmen, building workers and labourers.

One of the men who volunteered for the CCC was Jack McAulay, who worked on projects all over Australia.

> The men of the CCC did a wonderful job for the Australian and US forces during World War II. We carried out their building requirements all over Australia, particularly in northern parts. It was just like being in the forces because you had to go wherever they sent you.

Jack worked on the building of the American Headquarters in Brisbane so the US personnel could transfer from Melbourne to Queensland.

> It took about 200 of us a few months to complete this project and we were camped at the Brisbane suburb of Chermside. The Australian Army and the CCC camps adjoined one another. We were driven to work by Australian and US trucks in convoy led by a few motor cycle dispatch riders. They drove ahead of the convoy and held up the traffic, including the trams, so we could get to our job quickly. The US forces wanted their new headquarters as soon as possible.

Jack McAulay, second from left, back row, with members
of a CCC crew at Victoria Park, Brisbane, in June 1943.

The project was supervised by a US Army officer who had been an architect in America.

Among other projects I worked on was accommodation for the Australian Navy at Nelson Bay at Port Stephens. After we finished the job the Navy took over till the war's end and in 1947 it was used by migrants who came out from Europe to settle in Australia.

We worked at Merrylands in Sydney where we built a hospital at Merrylands Park for sick and wounded US forces. They arrived at the railway station and were put into a siding from which they were transported by US ambulances the short distance to the hospital.

Among other jobs I worked on were accommodation at Dapto for the RAAF, store rooms at Regents Park for the RAAF, storage igloos at Rydalmere on the Parramatta River for the Australian Navy, and warehouses for the US Army adjacent to the railway lines at Lichfield and Rozelle.

In Townsville again he built warehouses for the US forces at Aitkenvale, quarters for the WAAAF (Women's Australian Auxiliary Air Force) at Rosslea and other jobs for the US Army Air Forces.

Security was pretty tight while working on the US Army Air Forces base at Mount Louise.

We had to sleep on the base, were issued with special identity cards and had our fingerprints taken by US security personnel. I've never seen so many aircraft with about 500 Liberator bombers on the base.

On one job in Townsville the CCC worked alongside a group of civilians from Hong Kong.

They'd been taken prisoner by the Japanese and were being shipped to Japan when they were intercepted and rescued by the US Navy and brought to Australia.

It was so hot during summer in Townsville that the Americans decided to build their own ice works. They used to put blocks of ice into canvas water bags that held about 10 gallons [45 litres] each and hung them around the building sites and all their camps where thousands of troops and airmen were stationed.

It was while working on projects for the US forces that Jack first encountered chainsaws.

It was a real eye-opener for us to work with these chain saws to cut the stumps to do the building.

Jack says that others he knew in the CCC worked in Darwin, Karumba, Jackie Jackie and Iron Range.

We were known as the Army behind the Army by the defence chiefs, but the men of the CCC always reckoned we were the Army ahead of the Army, as we had to go ahead and build the camps, hospitals, warehouses, igloos and roads ready for the defence forces to occupy.

But despite the important work they were doing and the fact that they were all issued with numbers similar to Army personnel, they received few, if any, of the advantages of being in the forces.

Our own camps were very poor, some of them having only hurricane lamps. There were cold showers, no sewers, no army rations, no amenities and no camp concerts or travelling picture shows. However, the Army used to let us in to watch their shows if there were any nearby.

The men in the CCC had to provide their own work clothes, boots and their own good clothes and blankets. The Government of the day provided the absolute bare minimum for us. We slept on old stretchers with hessian bags filled with straw for mattresses and the pillows were made of the same material.

We had to provide all our own tools and we even had to provide the files to keep our handsaws sharp. If we lost or damaged a tool we had to buy a replacement. We had to buy our own soap, toothpaste, hair oils etc and when we moved camp we were loaded up like packhorses with our tool kits and a couple of rolled up blankets tied to our suit cases.

There were no medical services in our camp, unlike the Army. They provided the meals but we had to pay for them and the money was docked from us each pay day.

Jack said the girls in the Land Army were provided with overalls, a uniform to wear, a big hat to protect them from the sun and were later allowed to take part in the Anzac Day march. Nothing like this was available to members of the CCC.

One aspect of the work that Jack found disappointing was the fact that the men were split up at the end of each project.

We would be sent to different projects with a different gang of men all the time, unlike the army units who stayed together. We could not establish real friendships with the other men as you would just get to know each other and then a transfer of labour could see you 50 to 100 miles away with a different gang of men.

We received a Civilian Service Medal and certificate 50 years after the war ended. The certificate states in part, 'A grateful nation expresses its thanks to Daniel John McAulay for contributing to the war effort and the coming of peace.'

But I often wonder how grateful they were really.

Supplied by Jack McAulay of New South Wales

REWARDING AND WORTHWHILE LIFE IN THE WOMEN'S LAND ARMY

Isobel Anstee
Australian Women's Land Army
Victoria 1943–1944

ne of the most important industrial products during World War II was flax. It was used for all sorts of clothing and equipment, from coats to parachute harnesses, ropes to tarpaulins and even to cover gliders used to transport troops.

When the British Government lost its traditional flax supplies from Russia, Belgium and Ireland, it was forced to look elsewhere and sent stocks of flax seed to Australia to fill the gap.

Meanwhile, the Australian Women's Land Army (AWLA) was formed in 1942 to find replacements for the farming men who had joined the services. The government constantly found itself at odds with farmers who were seeking the release from the defence forces of their former workers in order to meet war production contracts. Recruiting women to replace them went much of the way to solving the problem.

Picking apples and grapes or testing herds of cattle, it was all the same to Isobel Anstee. As a member of the AWLA, she was called on to do a number of different jobs.

> In my case, I picked apples in the country town of Ringwood, then I was sent to the Chateau Tahbilk to pick grapes and then on to Lake Bolac to work with the flax.

But arrangements were not always perfectly made and the girls were often called upon to use their initiative in order to find their way to the jobs.

> I remember when sent to Bolac, my friend and I were dropped off at a lonely railway station approximately 4 feet by 8 feet [1.2 m x 4.2 m], just enough for two girls and two cases. We looked around—no sign of anyone to meet us, just miles of flat brown earth in every direction.

Isobel Anstee at work on the farm.

So we sat on our cases and later were picked up by a truck where we had to stand in the back with our cases. It was a very bumpy ride.

Eventually we arrived at our hostel where we were to work—approximately 30 cabins with two girls to each cabin and an old farm house where we had our meals.

Her work in the flax mills at Lake Bolac was the most important job she did during the war. It was also the hardest. The hours were long and the job entailed working in dusty conditions.

Britain sent 400 tonnes of flax seed to Australia where it was grown in Tasmania, Victoria, South Australia and Western Australia.

The Land Army was formed on the model of the British Land Army with the object of stepping up production of flax fibre, mainly for Britain, as well as food products and many other crops for canning. These products were for the fighting forces and also for export and there was a very great shortage of help to harvest the crops.

From 1942 to 1945 the strongest claim for help was for flax work. No soldier's coats or packs etc could be made without linen thread. The RAAF needed parachute harnesses all made with linen thread. The RAN needed canvas ropes, so did the Merchant Navy.

Canvas hosepipes were needed by the ARP and civilian fire brigades. Tents and tarpaulins were needed for all services.

The Aussie flax producing the parachute harness and fire hoses complied with strict specifications of the British Admiralty and was used extensively also for covering gliders for the D Day landing and parachute drop into Normandy.

They soon found that the often untrained help possessed initiative and ability to stand long hours in all weather. The women also adapted themselves to the isolation of jobs of many assignments.

Recruits for the AWLA were assessed for fitness and we had to accept the condition that we must go when and where directed. Our uniform was exactly the same as the AWAS [Australian Women's Army Service]. Our hours were 28 days work with two days off each month (and nowhere to go).

My two years spent in the Land Army were very rewarding and worthwhile.

I picked apples, grapes and stooked oats. I went on to the flax mill at Lake Bolac, where approximately 60 girls worked.

We spread flax and sometimes worked in the flax mill. The hours were long and it was hard and dusty work.

Isobel was asked to work on the weigh-bridge for a season where she was expected to assess the quality of the flax loads coming in—A, B or C grades.

While at Bolac, we had severe bush fires which threatened our flax stacks. The girls took tea and sandwiches to the firefighters and camped in the ashes overnight, where it was comparatively safe. Some people lost their lives during these fires, but thankfully, no Land Army girls

Despite the long working hours, the girls were still able to put on a great concert in the local hall at Lake Bolac during 1943.

Isobel's next assignment was to attend a crash course in herd testing at Burnley Agricultural College.

I bought an old car, a Chenard Walker, which had gate gears outside the cabin near the running board, and drove from Melbourne to Leongatha in Gippsland—learning to drive on the way. I was responsible for testing herds in a 10-mile [16 km] radius of Leongatha.

When I was demobbed I was exhausted. I met Corporal John Tipping who was recovering from his war experiences in New Guinea. He was hospitalised at the Heidelberg Military Hospital for three months and I was warned that he would have trouble in his middle years. We married and had three beautiful children, but he died at the age of 44 years.

Isobel was a widow for seven years until she married Captain William Ballard. They were married for 25 years until his death in January 2001.

Supplied by Isobel Ballard of Victoria

Patons Service Woollies

Specialty Knitting Book No. 153

A Patons & Baldwins' Publication - 7D

Knitters of Australia
Civilians
1935–1945

 any a mother, sister, aunt or girlfriend spent hours during World War II knitting woollen clothes for servicemen.

The garments were added to comfort parcels sent anonymously, on the whole, to servicemen at the front or who had been taken prisoner of war. Sometimes the knitter or parcel packer would slip in a note with good wishes and her address in the hope of receiving a reply—and many did.

So much knitting was required that special knitting groups were formed. While some women were accomplished knitters, others were new to the game and found great help from publications produced by companies specialising in patterns for a huge range of woollen garments.

One such booklet was *Patons Service Woollies, Specialty Knitting Book No 153*, produced by Patons and Baldwins of Melbourne and Sydney, which cost seven pence. It contained advice on knitting for those with less experience and detailed instructions for some of the more unusual garments.

Knitters! Please Take Notice

Avoid disappointment—buy the wool recommended. Buy wisely—buy enough—the same blend cannot be repeated. Tension is the number of stitches in width to measure one inch. On this depends the success of the finished article. If the tension is not obtainable on the needles recommended, use a size finer or coarser, as required.

Section 1 was devoted to service comforts such as pullovers. It featured a variety of styles, such as the Bruce—a V-neck with sleeves for army personnel, the

Cover of Pattons Service Woollies Knitting Book.

Franklin—another V-neck for air force personnel and the Keith—a crew neck for naval personnel. There were also sleeveless pullovers, a waistcoat with buttons and a cardigan.

Next came the neck comforts: scarves and neck muffs, balaclava helmets both with and without scarves, and sleeping caps. There were socks of all shapes and sizes, including some without toes and heels, some with Dutch heels, others with French heels and some with a flat toe. There were glove patterns with individual fingers and steering gloves without fingers. Mittens and wristlets were also popular.

Then there were specialised items in hospital comforts, many designed specifically for the wounded, such as a convalescent jacket with only half a back. Hospital stockings came with and without feet, and there were special patterns for hospital sleeves, knee covers, heel-less bed socks and a hot water bag cover. All came with detailed instructions on wool and needle sizes and advice on casting off to ensure the garments were as well made as possible.

When parcels arrived at the front or in POW camps, many a recipient was grateful for the warmth and comfort provided by these garments that had been so lovingly made by the womenfolk back home.

Written by Tony Miller from the Patons booklet

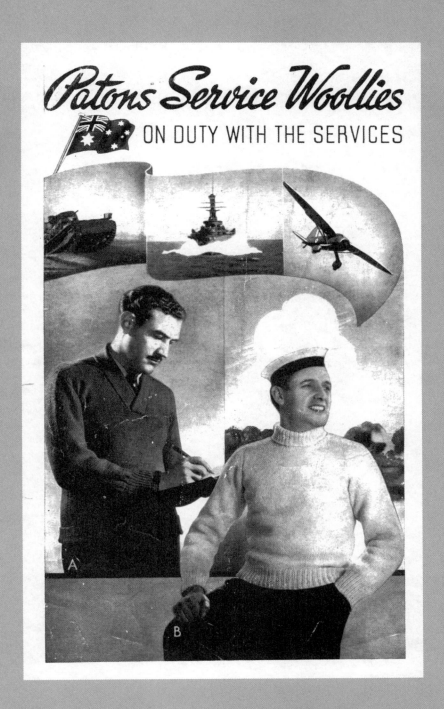

'1236 DIVER CUT SAIGON–SINGAPORE CABLE'

Sub-Lieutenant Ken Briggs
Royal Australian Naval Volunteer Reserve
French Indochina (Vietnam) July 1945

It seems hard to believe that a piece of cable 45 cm long could have a profound effect on the outcome of the war, but that's how it was.

As part of Operation Sabre, Sub-Lieutenant Ken Briggs, a diver, cut the piece from the Japanese underwater communications cable linking Saigon and Singapore. He was operating from a midget submarine in the Saigon River on 31 July 1945.

With the underwater cable out of action, the Japanese were forced to send their traffic by radio, enabling the US Navy to decode the signals. The Americans had cracked the Japanese military codes early in the Pacific war, which had given them a major advantage in the sea battles that followed.

Because the US Navy was intercepting all Japanese radio communications and gaining access to their plans, the Japanese began routing all sensitive communications through its submarine cable network.

It was then decided to cut the underwater cables—but this was easier said than done.

As it happened, the end of the war in Europe had freed up the top secret midget submarines the Royal Navy had used to attack German targets such as the battleship *Tirpitz*. The midget subs were transported to Australia in crates on the deck of a depot ship, HMS *Bonaventure*, ending up in Brisbane.

When Operation Sabre was set up to attack the underwater cables that linked Saigon with Singapore and Hong Kong, Sub-Lieutenant Ken Briggs was one of those selected to take part.

Sub-Lieutenant Ken Briggs in diving gear.

Briggs, who hailed from Glenn Innes, had joined the Royal Australian Naval Volunteer Reserve (RANVR) straight from school in 1941 as an ordinary seaman 2nd class. He was trained as an anti-submarine detection (ASDIC) operator and then sent to Britain along with 15 colleagues.

After serving with British forces on motor launches in the Mediterranean, he was recommended for a commission and returned to England for training.

After that he was transferred to the top secret midget submarines. These normally had a crew of three—the commander, navigator and engineer—but they often operated with the addition of a diver who was needed for jobs such as attaching limpet mines to the hulls of enemy shipping or cutting anti-submarine nets guarding harbours.

Ken was one of two divers who crowded into the tiny submarine, XE4, on 30 July 1945, lying on top of the batteries for most of the 30 hours or so that the expedition lasted. It had been towed to the area by a full-sized submarine, HMS *Spearhead*, to within 170 km of the Vietnamese coast before setting off under its own power. It towed a grappling hook with which they hoped to snag the cable.

After one false alarm when the hook caught on a rock, it finally seemed to hook onto the underwater cable.

Ken and colleagues on a midget submarine in Scotland.

Ken Briggs went through the procedure of flooding the wet-dry chamber in which he was travelling, then exited the submarine to check the line. To his delight, he found they had caught onto the thick cable and he returned to the sub for the air-powered cutters necessary to cut through it. This part of the operation took barely more than 10 minutes.

Ken Briggs' mission accomplished, he took the 45 cm piece he had cut out of the cable and re-entered the submarine.

The ship's operation report described the event in unemotional language.

> 1229 Diver out (S/Lt Briggs)
> 1236 Diver cut Saigon–Singapore cable
> 1242 Diver in with short length of cable as evidence
> 1250 Proceeded on course

With half the job done, the crew went looking for the Saigon–Hong Kong cable. Again they were lucky and a second diver had the honour of cutting this one. Then it was back to their towing submarine and then their depot ship in Labuan.

The US Army hailed the successful expedition. Military command were preparing to drop the atomic bomb on Hiroshima and were desperate to have access to Japanese cable traffic again.

Ken Briggs was awarded the Distinguished Service Cross (DSC) for his exploits.

Supplied by Ken Briggs of Queensland

'OUR HELL ON EARTH'

Sergeant Reg Mahoney
8th Division, Australian Imperial Force
Prisoner of War

E ach day Australian soldiers captured by the Japanese spent as prisoners of war they longed for freedom. They thought about family and friends at home and just hoped to survive for the end of the war.

When victory finally arrived they had mixed feelings, however. Many of those who had suffered at the hands of the Japanese were euphoric. Others were too ill to really enjoy the moment. But then frustration set in for some as they waited to be released. They were told for their own safety to stay put until Allied troops arrived at their camp.

Reg Mahoney had been in Changi and various camps in Thailand. During that time he kept a diary, writing on any scrap of paper he could get hold of. He buried the diary to avoid detection and almost certain death from Japanese guards. He dug up the diaries and took them with him each time they moved camp.

When the war ended, one of his first actions was to write a long letter to his brother, Jim, describing his feelings.

> Dear Jim, It's great to be free. Tho' we are still living as POWs in crowded bamboo huts, eating rice and stew, there is meat in the stew and we will soon be living like white men once again. At last we have a radio and transmitter in camp and at least get some news, but are very much in the dark. Heard today that NCOs including Australians have left Bangkok by plane for Rangoon. I expect to see some movement after all these surrenders are signed. Its reported they are going to Bangalore, India, tho' why the Australians should go there has us puzzled. However, we've been mucked around for 3 years by the Nips and must not squeal about our own administration having a go at us for a few months.

Soldiers celebrate being freed from a POW camp.

Three Yank paratroops arrived here yesterday and were truly embarrassed by the mob's curiosity to look at a free man. It was a great shock to every one of us to learn that our troops were in the country. They praise the Thais 5th column support. Our experiences with Thais in 43 and 44 led us to regard them as treacherous, the average being capable of selling a man for a few dollars. But their attitude noticeably changed in the latter end of last year.

Most of us are fairly fit now and a much better sight than the drafts of scarecrows when I left the Jungle two years ago. How is everyone at home? We're proud to hear of the part our boys have played and its useless trying to express our gratitude for being released from our hell on earth. Every one of us realize how lucky we are to get out alive. H.Q., R.A.A. has been split about. As far as I know, we only lost one—Phil Hunter, missing after a bombing at Bangkok while coming to this camp on 27 March. His mate, Keith Trayhurn, lost a foot, but is in fine fettle here. I've never seen a lad with more guts. Phil Kelly, also is here, Chas Kelly in Bangkok.

Have had 28 letters or cards from you, Mum, Dad, Jean, Babs and Fred. Thank you all for the brightest spots in 3 years. And three snaps were never worth more to anyone. We are sweating now for more mail, papers and evidence of a white man's world.

Our cry once was 'If only we were free' but this waiting is harder to bear than we expected. The novelty of working freely with no coolie work under our barbaric hosts is beginning to wear off and who can blame the boys for getting on the Thai whisky, kin to metho? Have no inclination for it myself. There are thousands of Nips in the area. They still have the guns and we are unarmed, but, fortunately; there have been no serious incidents since the peace, despite much drunken A.W.L. [Absent Without Leave] taunting from both this and the officers' camp nearby.

Nacom Nai village is about six miles from here, but there and back is nothing after all the marching we've done—three or four miles to work and back every day—1 to 2 hours on our feet (mostly bare) rice and stew for meals.

When the Yank paratroop medical orderly drew his chow last night, he cried: 'God, you guys been living on this?' Ho, that's 100 per cent better than we've been living on for 3 years. 'That's just shit,' he said, throwing out the rice and stew, thick with meat, veg. and beans. He walked to his kit and opened a tin of bully and biscuit. God knows what he'd have said about our Jungle 'pap' or melon water.

Later, on his return to Australia, Reg Mahoney wrote more about his experiences under the Japanese. He recalled two incidents that were particularly memorable. The first occurred at Changi Beach in Singapore in 1942.

We drew shovels and chunkles (the heavy hoe which is the all purpose digging tool of the Orient) and marched towards the beach. Conjecture was rife on the nature of our job.

We are going to start gardens, declared the practical minded among us.

'Maybe the Japs are looking for something that's been buried, and we are to dig the Island up, til they find it,' said one romantic minded chap.

'Yes, perhaps the gold and silver that was dumped into the sea from the banks,' came a forlorn voice.

One sarcastic joker jarred our nerves by remarking, 'Well by the look of that Nip's fiendish face we may be going to dig our own graves.'

'Shut your morbid trap,' he was told.

Sergeant Reg Mahoney in uniform.

'Anyway they had best give us a feed if they expect us to do much work.'

'My oath,' was the popular reply.

We passed through a grove on the edge of the beach and halted. Everyone turned to gaze out on the sea, calm and serene.

'My God, look there!' exclaimed someone pointing to the edge of the water.

Yes, we were looking at and stood horror-stricken by what was 'there'.

Bobbing on the gentle swell and fall of the water were cloth covered blobs, unmistakably the bodies of men.

They seemed to be everywhere. Gruesome patches of human dead, blotching the edge of the water as it lapped the pure sand of the beach. Figures in grotesque positions with arms and legs askew, upturned faces white in the sun, faces sunk in the sand or water.

Each man slowly turned his eyes from this sight towards the faces of the Jap guards. There was one thought in each mind—'You bloody murdering swine!'

As though they read this thought, the Japs gruffly globbered at us and sorted us out to work.

We started digging, obviously the excavation was a big grave for the bodies that lay on the beach.

It was hard work in our weakened state, made worse by the mental strain caused by the nature of the job. Try as we would, we could not prevent our eyes from wandering towards the beach, wondering what those bodies were and what devilry was behind their death.

Then came the gruesome job of dragging the corpses to the grave. To make this worse, we found that their hands had been tied together, and the victims linked in fives or sixes.

As we expected, they were Chinese, mostly wearing coarse blue clothes. We could not tell whether some were young men or women.

Troops on board ship heading for Asia.

There were bullet holes in different parts of the bodies.

It was easy to imagine the scene. To create terror and leave no doubt as to who wore the iron heel, the Japs had rounded up these Chinese, perhaps selecting at random, and brought them to the beach.

Tied together the Chinese had been marched into the sea and callously slaughtered with a burst of machine gun fire in their backs.

The perpetration of this act on the beach near our camp, and the selection of POWs to bury the bodies, no doubt, was to impress us.

Sweat pouring from us under the tropic sun, we lumbered the corpses to the grave, and dumped them in with sickening thuds. They fell in all sorts of weird positions, limbs buckled under bodies, an arm or hand upflung as though in shameful appeal against such a fate.

At first we tried to make the burial as decent as possible by placing the bodies straight. Such a nicety was quickly prevented by the Jap guards, who ghoulishly seemed to want the job done as gruesomely as possible.

One man was dragging bodies from the water's edge when he started back with a strained grim face and blazing eyes to shout—'Jesus, this one is still alive!'

He was joined by others who began to examine the body, in which there were unmistakable signs of life.

A Jap rushed to the scene, kicked the body, and then made signs for it to be held under the water. The men quietly stood there refusing to move. He swung his rifle forward and made ready for a bayonet lunge at the nearest man's belly. Slowly the men moved to the sickly task. We were forced to render similar treatment on other bodies in which life was suspected.

'The Japs must pay for this,' was the determination expressed by every man present.

Approximately 120 bodies were buried there, and we wondered how many more may have been slaughtered in other places.

When we had finished the task, disgusted in mind and sick in body, we wearily marched back to camp.

Even the thought of food did not have the same appeal to us that night.

Another example of brutality involved the POWs at Hintok Mountain Camp during the Big Purge on the Burma–Thailand Railway in 1943.

> The five men missing from No. 2 gang when the check was made, were called out and stood to attention. 'Molly the Monk', a lumbering heavy individual, strode up and punched each man twice in the face. He was followed by his corporal, 'Jumbo'. Two men were knocked down. The Japs kicked them viciously until they groggily stood up.
>
> This was a real 'Roman Holiday' for the Japs, who excitedly babbled among themselves, and jeered at the prisoners.
>
> The sight of cruelty always seemed to have an influence on Japanese passion, and tonight they were all keyed up for the occasion. Each one impatiently waited his turn to rush in and hit a victim in the face, kick him or throw him with 'ju-ju'.
>
> Two men were knocked unconscious and could not rise. In a wicked fury the Japs kicked them, tore at their ears and hair and tried to make them stand up. Then they jumped up and down on the bodies, cursing and spitting.
>
> This was a display of pure animalism, there was no drink or drug to blame for the bestiality that showed itself in the Japanese character.
>
> Two of our officers arrived on the scene to protest, but they were driven off with pick handles.
>
> While this barbaric scene was unfolding; our gang (No 1) was standing to attention, three men short, and the sergeant in charge had been sent off to find them.
>
> When the Japs were satisfied that the first five men had been punished, they dismissed No 2 gang and the men carried the victims away.
>
> Then the Japs turned to us, and told us we would stay there until the three missing men turned up. They asked us if anyone knew who the missing men were, but after seeing what had happened to the others, nobody was willing to tell them. We agreed it would be better to stand there all night than see another such display of cruelty.
>
> The sergeant returned to say he could not find the missing men. The Japs told him if he did not bring them he and the rest of us would be flogged.

Immediately they heard of this, the three missing men came forward, although they had heard the Jap's shrieks while venting their sadistic fury, on others. Those three men were bashed, kicked, thrown, jumped on and pummelled for an hour and a half. When the Japs could not knock them out, they tried to throw them into the fire.

When the punishment stopped the three men were stood to attention. They stood there, faces black with bruises, eyes swollen, and bodies covered with red weals, and, although their knees were shaking the very set of their heads and shoulders spelled defiance and contempt. Their spirit was magnificent. Their names were Corporal Alan Hourigan, Sapper 'Squeaker' Worther, and Corporal Wimpie.

It was almost midnight when we were dismissed, and, unable to break the spirit of the three men, the Japs ordered them to work the next day.

One of the men beaten up, Sergeant Mick Hallam of Tasmania, died the following day, and two others were left with permanent injuries.

There was not a man in the camp who did not swear vengeance on that gang of engineers, but I suppose when the war finished they were in another part of the East, perhaps ingratiating themselves with the suave smile of the Japanese, upon their supposedly temporary captors.

Supplied by Reg Mahoney of New South Wales

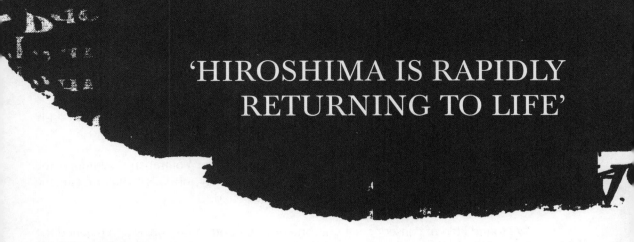

'HIROSHIMA IS RAPIDLY RETURNING TO LIFE'

Sergeant Eric Saxon
Combined Services Detailed Interrogation Centre
British Commonwealth Occupation Force
Japan 1946–1947

ric Saxon was a happy and relieved man when he sailed into Kure Harbour in Japan on 9 April 1946 with the British Commonwealth Occupation Force (BCOF).

The voyage from Australia on MV *Duntroon* had been full of drama. There was an emergency dash to port with a dangerously ill soldier, then later the ship had to withstand typhoons and endure a shortage of water. The journey, which should have taken just a couple of weeks, lasted four weeks.

> As we were driven through Kure I was impressed by the crowded streets, the very heavy bomb and fire damage, the number of bicycles and the many unaccustomed smells—food, dried fish, garbage and so on. There was an odd mixture of western and Japanese dress, most working women wearing mompei (a sort of loose baggy trousers).

New members of the Combined Services Detailed Interrogation Centre (CSDIC) were required to attend a 12-week intensive Japanese course, something Eric took to with relish, particularly as he had already studied Japanese for his role in intelligence activities during World War II. At the end of the course, CSDIC members were attached to various units as official interpreters.

Before leaving his native Tasmania, Eric contacted the editor of the *Hobart Mercury*, suggesting he could write some articles for the paper while he was in Japan. As he was not a journalist, the editor was non-committal but agreed he would look at what he sent through. In the end, the paper published more than 20 of his articles, which were attributed to 'A Special Correspondent with the British Occupation Force in Japan'.

Supervising Japanese soldiers.

Once he completed his language training, Eric was thrown into a maelstrom of unfamiliar tasks as an interpreter with 36 Field Security Section at Onomichi.

Our duties involved trips through the district in a jeep to interrogate people suspected of being involved in smuggling or other illegal activities.

One operation involved boarding a ship to search for contraband. Although the boarding party was armed, I carried no weapons. My job was to interrogate the captain and others while the ship was being searched.

We found little of consequence but somehow a report on the operation reached the Australian press where it was blown out of all proportion. The headline was 'Australian Troops Seize Vessel in Onomichi Port' or something like that. In reality it was a very low key exercise.

One of Eric's early articles for the *Mercury* referred to the devastation at Hiroshima.

Early in August 1945, Hiroshima was in the headlines of every newspaper in the world. Much has happened since then but the day of the first terrific demonstration to the world of the tremendous energy in the atom will long be remembered everywhere. It will probably be remembered for ever in this part of Japan.

Recently I have seen Hiroshima two or three times and have seen what modern war can mean. On approaching the city, the first visible effects of the blast are seen in the tiles on the roofs, which are moved as if some giant hand had swept them from their places. At first only a few here and there are moved but on going further into the city, more and more are swept away, uncovering woodwork underneath.

Then the plaster on the walls is missing here and there, so that the bamboo slats underneath are revealed. Further on again whole roofs have fallen in and walls have jagged gaps. Most of these houses still have people living in them but only a few have been repaired. By the time the first branch of the river is reached, the houses which remain lean shakily. Many have been demolished.

Across the river there is utter destruction as the tremendous fires which started in the centre of the city spread through areas only partly destroyed by the blast, and were stopped by the various river mouths. The outskirts, both east and west, are similar and from the lean on houses, and twisted iron framework, it is possible to judge where the bomb struck.

In the centre of the city there is complete desolation—piles of rubble, rusting tins and ironwork, masses of fused metal and glass, including the scarcely recognisable framework of tram cars, bicycles, cars and sewing machines.

Trees are merely charred stumps while steel electric standards heel over at every angle. Many concrete and brick buildings still stand but are burned out inside. Some have been moved on their foundations.

However, Hiroshima is rapidly returning to life. Sawmills for miles around are working overtime and scores of wooden buildings are springing up among the ruins.

Open air stalls display their wares and attract large crowds. Trams are running, crowded to capacity.

When he wrote the article Eric was concerned that this work was being done in a haphazard fashion.

Yet no plan seems to exist for the reconstruction so that the new buildings probably will become the nucleus for future slums. Very little cleaning up by the municipal authorities has been done but individuals have made shacks of old iron and scraps among the ruins and have planted gardens in areas they have cleared of rubble.

No one seems to have the strength or will to undertake the rebuilding of the city on modern lines, so in the future they may expect worse congestion than in the past.

Troops arrive at Kure, Japan, on MV *Duntroon*, 9 April 1946.

Hiroshima paid a terrific price to bring the war to a more speedy end. The fate of tens of thousands who perished in its ruins, by convincing the Japanese Government of the futility of continuing the war, saved the lives of perhaps hundreds of thousands on both sides.

For this, those now living who might well have died, owe something to the memory of Hiroshima, the city which suffered more severely in proportion than any other city in the world.

So while we may forgive its survivors their apathetic looks, especially after having seen the horrible scars left by atomic burns, we must never allow the world to forget its lesson.

Fortunately, Eric's fears for Hiroshima's future back in 1946 were not borne out as he discovered during subsequent visits to the area some years later.

He became involved in supervising the reception of Japanese soldiers and civilians coming back from China and South-East Asia and the repatriation of civilians to Okinawa and Korea.

Cholera was common among returning troops, so we had inoculations and lots of DDT was used to 'delouse' those in the large barracks where they were held while being officially discharged from the forces and despatched to their former home areas.

In another article in the *Mercury*, Eric wrote about the reactions of Japanese people to the foreign troops.

The reactions of the men are certainly the most difficult to understand. For the most part the men take little notice of troops passing through. Sometimes they continue their work as though nothing had happened; mostly they watch with expressionless faces.

In the country areas where troops pass only occasionally, the men frequently greet troops by smiling, raising their hats and bowing, or waving hoes or whatever they may happen to have in their hands.

The women are more actively friendly than the men and many of them, particularly those with children on their backs, wave vigorously to passing troops while their menfolk merely look on.

By far the most impressive feature of the attitude of Japanese towards the Allied forces is the behaviour of the children, more especially in rural areas where troops do not pass frequently.

The way these children greet the troops has to be seen to be believed, it is so overwhelming in its openheartedness and spontaneity. As a result, almost every Australian who has been in such areas is deeply touched and freely admits that he has 'a lot of time for the kids'.

One of the jobs carried out by the occupation forces was to enforce the ruling that schools abandon their militaristic teaching and that all books and other materials containing such material be destroyed.

Eric spent a lot of time at schools and talking to children.

As for the next generation, I am satisfied that the children are our way now, and that their friendship as adults depends entirely on the effectiveness of the new education system, and of the wisdom of the measures which must be taken by the Allied military governments of the future.

The first anniversary of the war's end, 15 August 1946, was a holiday for those BCOF troops who could be spared from duty. For the Japanese it was not such a celebration.

Today was also a general holiday for the Japanese, but for a rather different reason. Although they make no secret of the fact they are pleased the war is over, even though lost, they have not yet gone so far as to celebrate the anniversary by any special festivities.

Today happens to be the main day of the traditional Bonodori festival. During the day the Japanese showed no particular festive spirit, but most spent it in relaxation or in preparation for the evening festivities. [The festival is a Buddhist rite which extends from about 10 August to 15 August. On the last night the spirits of departed ancestors are invoked by the living and are believed to revisit the earth.]

The only open daylight demonstrations in this area were made by Koreans. There is a considerable Korean element in south-west Japan, an element which is now organised into the Association of Koreans Residing in Japan.

Headquarters of the Kure branch today was bedecked with Korean and Allied flags, streamers and other coloured materials, while a large notice proclaimed 'Congratulations to the Allied Forces on Victory. Cheers!'

Just before Christmas Eric experienced his first earthquake.

At 0420 hours I awoke amid a loud rumbling and shaking of the hut. One of my room mates shouted 'earthquake' and went outside. I sat up in bed but as I knew the hut was wooden and well constructed, being held together by bolts rather than nails, I considered it safer to stay inside rather than risk loose tiles falling on me as I went out the door.

As I looked out I saw what looked like lightning flashes across the sky but soon realised it was the high-tension power lines swaying and touching to create sheets of flame. Then all lights went out.

In the dark we could hear the nearby primary school buildings creaking loudly as they swayed with the movement of the ground. As the shaking lessened I put on my overcoat and boots and ventured outside. The air was still and filled with shouts and activity from the town. The excitement soon died down, so I went back to bed.

Damage to the immediate area was not great. But south of Shikoku there was major damage and thousands died from fires that broke out in the collapsed houses and from the tsunami (tidal wave) that swept from the nearby epicentre and hit the coast, completely destroying many villages.

In April 1947, elections were held in Japan and BCOF personnel were involved in supervising them.

It was our duty to observe the pre-election campaign activities and to visit as many polling booths as we could on election days. We also had to collect statistics on the numbers voting at each centre.

This election duty was the most interesting experience during my time in Japan. Katsuyama was very much a rural centre. It had sustained no war damage and was remote from industrial activity. Very few foreigners visited the area. In places we found we were the first ever seen there so we were the focus of considerable curiosity.

I tried hard to find any malpractice in the elections but could not.

One of Eric's most enduring memories of his stay in Japan was his interaction with the locals and, in particular, the children who were intrigued to be able to talk with a foreigner in their own language. He visited many schools, getting to know the teachers and children, and was often invited to attend special occasions at the schools.

Eric left Japan on 15 September 1947 at the end of his tour of duty and sailed via New Zealand to Sydney. Despite some rough weather on the way, it proved to be rather less eventful than the outward voyage 18 months earlier.

Supplied by Eric Saxon of Queensland

FLYING MUSTANGS
OVER KOREA

NCO Pilot P3 Milton Cottee
77 Squadron, Royal Australian Air Force
Korea 1950

ilton Cottee saw his first aircraft in 1931 or 1932 when he was five or six as it flew over his home at Murwillumbah in northern New South Wales. It was the mail plane flying to Brisbane.

This sighting intrigued him and his curiousity was further aroused two years later when he drove with his father and brother to a field nearby, where an aircraft had landed.

> Parked near the dusty unpaved road was a motley collection of cars, bicycles, horses and carts. Into the field some distance there was a crowd of people. In the centre of this crowd was a huge aeroplane having three big engines. Lindsay said, 'There it is— Smithy's Southern Cross'.

Some years later, Milton watched in awe as three fighters performed aerobatics at the Richmond airbase while tied together with tape. If there had been any doubt where his future interests lay, they were settled that day.

In 1941, at the age of 15, he joined the Air Training Corps.

> While a cadet with the Air Training Corps, I made two significant visits to RAAF bases. The first was to Richmond, NSW, from where I made my first flight. I recall that it was in an Avro Anson. I was intrigued and excited by the whole thing and this first flight did much to firm my resolution to join the RAAF as soon as I could.

Milton enlisted in October 1944, as soon as he was 18, and underwent basic training. But by then the war was winding down, so he did not undertake flying training. He returned to civilian life, and had begun studying engineering at university when a friend showed him an advertisement calling for applications from those interested in joining the RAAF on the first post-war flying training course.

A 77 Squadron Mustang in Korea.

Three of us, who had previously met as members of No 63 wartime course, decided to apply for re-entry to the RAAF. My thinking was that I could always complete an engineering degree later but I would never have another opportunity to learn to fly with the RAAF. I did not realise at the time just how advantageous that year of university engineering would later turn out to be.

Flying training took place at Point Cook and later in Sale, both in Victoria, and Milton gained his wings in August 1949. Soon afterwards he was posted to 77 Squadron flying Mustangs at Iwakuni in Japan as part of the British Commonwealth Occupation Force (BCOF).

Not long afterwards, on 25 June 1950, forces from North Korea invaded South Korea to start a war that led to a three-year involvement for Australian forces. Milton Cottee was soon in the thick of it.

The third mission on 6 July was a classic. We started out as a four aircraft formation with Squadron Leader Graham Strout leading but he had to abort. Flying Officer Ken McLeod, our number three, took over and P2 Les Reading and I headed for Korea with full tanks, six rockets and as always full gun bins containing 2040 rounds. The inner guns in each wing had 230 more rounds than the outers. We always stopped firing when we got down to two guns, keeping those 400 odd rounds for self defence.

Checking in through the newly established Joint Operation Centre on our 4-channel VHF radio, we were assigned to a 'mosquito' control aircraft wanting aircraft to strike a bridge to hold up a T-34 tank column advancing south along the main Seoul/Taejong highway at P'yongtaek. We thought we would not be very effective against a bridge but we were the only aircraft he could get. [The 'mosquito' was an American forward air controller that directed artillery and aircraft strikes.]

We did not know at the time that earlier that day two sections of four Mustangs had strafed a train near P'yongtaek, believing the train to be North Korean. It was a terrible blunder. The train was carrying reinforcements for the small US force trying to delay the advancing tanks. Fortunately the Mustangs concentrated on destroying the train and the casualties amongst the US Army soldiers were light.

Soon after contacting the mosquito aircraft—they were not yet called Forward Air Controllers (FACs)—Ken McLeod had us check our fuel state. We were close to bingo, a fuel state where we had only enough to get us back to base. Ken advised on the radio that we would only have a short time on target before having to return to base.

Still about 15 miles from the target the mosquito pilot suddenly called to us in a very agitated voice saying, 'Little Friends come hubba hubba I am being attacked.' He couldn't identify the attacking aircraft and continued to call for help. We all fire-

Australian troops arrive at Iwakuni.

A142

walled the throttles and rapidly ate up the distance between us. I turned on the master armament switch and set up the guns and gun-sight for air to air. I even fired off a few rounds to make sure all was good and ready.

My aircraft was a little faster than the others or maybe I had more RPM selected and hence more power. Speed kept increasing up towards 350 knots and soon I could make out the mosquito aircraft and then another type flying away down a valley as though to escape. I was closest to this aircraft and called my intention to go after it.

It didn't take long to close the gap for an almost dead line astern attack. I concentrated on centring the small dot of the gyro gun-sight on the target. The aircraft rapidly grew in size and I knew that with no deflection I could hardly miss. Just a few more seconds to close the range—and then I started to make out some features. A two seater with the person in the rear seat obviously having seen me and causing the pilot to try some evasive manoeuvres. One of these was a violent yaw to the right so that I could see markings on the right rear fuselage.

Instantly I recognised the markings as South Korean. My thoughts 'No red star here. Maybe it was a North Korean in South Korean markings. No firing now—but watch out he may try to shoot at me as I overshoot him—so don't give him a chance— overtake him to the right and get a good look followed by a tight left half barrel roll to slow down and keep him in sight from above. If he is quick, however, he may still be able to get a few shots off in my direction. Try to tell the others.'

I went to press my transmit button in the end of the throttle twist grip with my left thumb, only to find, to my dismay, that there was no button where it should have been!

By now I was alongside, with an overtaking speed of about 200 knots and I recognised it as a T-6 Harvard, like the Wirraways I had trained on. Still suspicious, I pulled away as the pilot of the Harvard vigorously rocked his wings. I then heard Les Reading call up and say with relish, 'Milt's missed him he's mine.'

And now I could look back and see Les lining up on the Harvard. How could I quickly tell him not to fire? I looked into the end of the throttle and saw that there were two contacts sitting there, where the little plastic push button used to be. I could see this on the floor of the cockpit but I couldn't reach it. I needed something to push those contacts together—but what? My fingers were too big. A pencil, which I always kept handy, served the purpose and I heard the radio click as it went to transmit. 'Les don't shoot—it's South Korean—Don't shoot.'

A split second later and that South Korean Harvard would have been a fireball.

Whilst Ken McLeod kept station above and to the rear of the Harvard, Les and I came back for a closer look, coming up on each side of the stranger. The poor fellow in the back was waving his arms in recognition as much as his canopy would allow and even the pilot in front was waving one hand in supplication. I waved back and confirmed him as South Korean.

Ken called us back into battle formation and we headed back towards where we had first seen the mosquito aircraft, berating the pilot more than somewhat for calling an enemy attack. Seems it had come at him out of the sun and given him a hell of a fright. They both had thought the other was an enemy.

Now we were past our bingo fuel and still had a target to attack. Ken conferred with the mosquito saying we could land at Pusan or Pohang if we had to. The FAC said, 'Aussies you have to hit that bridge down there and watch out for the tank column approaching it from the north. All friendlies have now crossed the bridge but they are being hard pressed by the tanks.'

Putting aside our predicament over fuel and a place to land we looked over the area. As we approached the bridge we could see the lead T34 tanks slowly moving down the road. Muzzle flashes from machine guns indicated they were firing at us. A few rounds from us and the tank column stopped, presumably to give them a better platform from which to fire back at us.

These were the tanks that had just routed Task Force Smith near Ansong, 12 miles [19 km] to the north, the first US army attempt to slow the advance. We did not know that beneath us at P'yongtaek the remnants of that brave task force of 406 men under Lieutenant Colonel Smith were straggling south as best they could. They had quickly found that their anti tank weapons had been almost ineffectual against the T34 tanks.

It was some time before we were to learn that we could easily knock out those tanks by firing our guns into the engine compartment behind the gun turret.

We soon assessed the best attacking direction on the bridge and made three runs firing two rockets on each pass. We hit the bridge a few times, with the tanks firing at us each time we came within range. The bridge was not knocked down but may have been severely weakened by our rockets with their 60 pound [27 kg] heads. Having each expended six rockets, our next concern was to find a place to land. It was already late in the afternoon and darkness was only 20 to 30 minutes away.

To our surprise the mosquito pilot called to invite us back to his airfield which turned out to be Taejon. He said it should be long enough for Mustangs and some fuel would be available. Ken opted for Taejon and we did lazy S turns over the aircraft as we escorted him back to Taejon. On going to Taejon tower frequency we soon found that it was coming home to roost time.

Light aircraft were converging on Taejon from all directions and already dusk was well advanced. A look down on Taejon showed a jumble of parked aircraft concentrated around a gravel strip. We were slotted into a long final with about eight aircraft ahead and others joining in behind. Through the deepening gloom I could see the other two Mustangs ahead picked out by their tail-lights and I touched down with three aircraft ahead still rolling on the strip. Hard braking stopped me from overrunning Les, who was also braking. Then into the first gap on my right and I was able to move clear by about 100 feet, where I ended up with my higher wings overlapping those of the smaller aircraft. I closed down and breathed a big sigh of relief.

Allied aircraft dominated the skies at this stage and were constantly called upon to support the ground forces.

Just north of the bomb line near Taegu were a few short railway tunnels. At night the North Koreans would use these tunnels to hide trucks loaded with supplies. We were assigned to attempt to make the tunnel entrances collapse using our rockets with their big 60 pound heads.

We found that the best attack could be made by flying just above the railway tracks approaching the tunnel entrance. A little pull-up to allow for gravity drop just before release of the rocket was required followed by a very hard pull to clear the hill above the tunnel entrance. This could be followed by a half roll to give one a view of the rocket explosion.

Using this technique about one in four rockets could be made to enter the tunnel. The resulting effects of the explosion of the rocket inside the tunnel was initially unexpected. There would be a whoosh of smoke out of the far end of the tunnel and a giant smoke ring would then come flying out of the near end.

After a couple of these we soon began a competition to blow the biggest and best smoke ring. For anyone or anything inside the tunnels it must have been decidedly unhealthy. The North Koreans soon stopped using those tunnels.

Other smoke rings were more ominous. These were from flak. I was never briefed on the finer points of flak until after a mission which took us over the harbour of Wonsan. Suddenly there were black puffs appearing about 5000 feet [1525 m] above us. Bay Adams called flak and to start weaving. He was already doing this quite vigorously and I started to do the same. However, I was intrigued that the flak continued to burst well above us, so my weaving dropped off.

During the debriefing after the mission Bay tore strips off me about my attempts at weaving. I exclaimed that the flak was way off target and nowhere near me. With raised eyebrows he said softly and with great effect, 'Is that the first time you have flown through self-destroying 40 mm?' It now dawned on me that the AA must have been passing close to me and that the proximity fuses may have come awfully close to finding me. Perhaps if I had been weaving more vigorously I may have flown closer to one of those nasty things.

As our war of interdiction developed we took on a close interest in a particular railway bridge across a ravine. Having knocked down this bridge early in the war we took the occasional opportunity to look at the attempts being made to rebuild it. About half way through its rebuild we went in and knocked it down again.

Flight Lieutenant Jack Murray and I, armed with rockets and guns, went in to have a look again, some time later. This time they were waiting for us. Soon after spotting the partially rebuilt bridge I saw two big black puffs of flak appear just behind Jack's aircraft. Soon after I felt the double thump from two bursts close to me. I recall a feeling of profound anger as I saw flashes from sandbagged gun emplacements near the bridge.

Being in a good position to roll immediately into a dive at one of the two AA guns, I brought my six 50 calibres to bear and opened up with a long hosing burst. Meanwhile, I selected rockets in salvo at minimum interval timing and flew in to the optimum launch range still firing my guns. Little figures were running in all directions around the AA gun I had selected as six rockets followed in close succession from my wings. Then followed a hard pull up and half roll to see the effects.

A few of the sandbags could still be seen but the gun had disappeared. As I rolled upright I spotted Jack diving on the remaining gun emplacement. Muzzle flashes showed that those on the ground had recovered from the surprise of my attack and were firing back, so I flew into position for a strafing dive in support. But this wasn't

A ricochet strike on the nose.

necessary. Jack's rockets streaked in onto the second gun emplacement and its ammunition went off with a huge smoking burst which reached up to engulf his aircraft. I was relieved to see him fly out of the smoke.

All signs of ground fire had now stopped. We were able to look over the partially rebuilt bridge without further interruption. Our report stated that the bridge would not need further attention for a while.

Two weeks later, a couple of well placed 500 pound bombs delivered during a 60 degree dive knocked the bridge down again.

Ground fire was the cause of most of the aircraft losses and damage, so it was always of concern.

Small calibre ground fire was ineffective whilst we were above about 1000 feet [305 m]. It was whilst strafing and firing rockets that we were most vulnerable. It was then also that we were able to see the muzzle flashes of ground fire. Without muzzle flashes there was no other indication to enable us to know that we were being fired at. That is, unless one took a hit. Even then it would have to be a hit which could be felt or which had damaging effect.

On 15 October our section of four, led by Flight Lieutenant Fred Barnes, was assigned to provide close support to Australian troops advancing into the village of Namchonjom. On arrival in the area we could see the Australian force advancing along a road about two miles [3.2 km] from the village. The road went straight through rice paddy fields, which were partly flooded with water. Enemy fire was coming from the village and the ground controller was soon asking us to subdue this fire.

We had napalm and guns and proceeded to drop our napalm on gun positions near the village. Following Fred out of his napalm run I was intrigued to see that he had a napalm tank hang-up under his left wing.

These hang-ups occasionally happened with the Japanese manufactured drop tanks we used. The two suspension lugs used to hang the tanks on the bomb racks had been made with slightly incorrect dimensions with the lugs a fraction too close together. This caused the tanks to sometimes jam on the bomb release unit. To get a positive release it became our practice to give the stick a hard sharp pull back at the moment of pressing the release button on the top of the stick.

Fred had done this but this tank was reluctant to come off. Another practice was for us to climb away from a target towards our own lines whenever possible. So I watched as Fred climbed up over our own troops. As he reached about 3000 feet and approaching our own troops, that tank came off. I watched in fearful apprehension as the tank of napalm tumbled end over end towards them, to land with a great burst of flame in a paddy field about 200 yards [180 m] off the road.

Fred's apologies to the ground controller were short as we carried on with strafing the enemy in the village. It was satisfying to see those Aussie troops occupy the village with the enemy retreating.

We flew often in direct support of troops on the ground. Mostly we were able to talk by radio to a ground controller who would direct our efforts for maximum effect.

Once whilst firing into enemy positions across a ravine, we received a call from the ground controller to make our attacks from another direction. He had just been hit on the back of his helmet by one of our cartridge cases. We had given little thought to the fact that our empties and links were being ejected overboard during gun firing.

On 20 October 1950 I flew a mission out of Pohang and landed at Kimpo about 30 minutes after dark. I recall touching down and rolling over a rough part of runway knowing that the roughness was a filled-in bomb crater, quite probably one I had earlier caused when I dropped two bombs on that same runway. We had also napalmed and strafed the Kimpo terminal building during successive missions. Now we found ourselves in the strange situation where we had to spend the night in that burned and beaten up terminal building.

The next day we were to give close support to one of the largest paradrops of the war in the Sukchong/Sunchon area south of Pyongyang. The troops were members of the 187th Airborne Regiment, understood to have been the first US Army troops deployed from the US in support of the Korean War. The Japanese gave them the nickname Rakkasans on their arrival in Japan.

We were up at first light and there, scattered over every available parking space, were C-82/C-119 Packets and C-47 Gooney Birds loading up with paratroopers and equipment. I took a few photographs before climbing into my fully armed Mustang wondering about the apprehension of all those brave men. I wanted so much to be as effective as possible in helping them.

Loading 500-pound bombs on a Mustang aircraft.

We watched from our cockpits as streams of these aircraft took off and formed up into huge formations. I took a few pictures. After they had all taken off, it was our turn and our 12 Mustangs took off to catch up with the transports.

We took up top cover positions above the huge formations. Soon they were disgorging thousands of parachutes on the selected drop zones. Airborne air controllers were already in position to direct our close support. We were soon hard at work suppressing sporadic ground fire from enemy troops. Often we found ourselves dodging around parachutes and giving encouraging waves to those descending. The enemy ground fire was short lived as we took every opportunity to pick off machine gun positions.

The paratroopers could be seen getting organised on the ground. Varied colours of parachutes were spread all over the ground like mushrooms. I was elated to have been able to provide direct covering fire for the descending troopers, some of whose lives may have been preserved as a result. Complete surprise seemed to have been achieved and this force did much to cut off large sections of the enemy as it was attempting to escape the trap that the Inchon landing turned out to be.

All of our 12 aircraft recovered to Pohang, some with minor hits from ground fire. We then busied ourselves with preparations for further missions in support of the Rakkasans the next day.

Milton Cottee's tour of duty came to an end when he completed 50 missions with a flight time of 150 hours. He returned to Australia. He went on to become one of very few to have served in World War II, Korea, Malaya and Vietnam, eventually retiring from the RAAF as a group captain.

Supplied by Milton Cottee of the ACT

Private Cyril 'Frenchy' Ray
Sniper, 2nd Battalion, The Royal Australian Regiment
Korea 1953

eing a sniper is a lonely job. Naturally, you are hated by the enemy, but your own troops sometimes also have a distaste for what you do.

'Frenchy' Ray was so called by his friends because he was born in Paris. He was recruited in England and volunteered to be a sniper in the Korean War to avoid having to undergo another period of basic training. He told the interviewing panel in Australia that he had been a sniper in the Parachute Regiment, so they were delighted to have him.

He joined three other snipers, Eddie McMahon from Adelaide and two brothers, Hugh and Kevin Tupper, from Brisbane. They were issued with a special heavy barrel 303 rifle with telescopic sights and were sent to Korea. Frenchy Ray fired five bullets from his sniper rifle before embarking with the 2nd Battalion, The Royal Australian Regiment (2RAR) in March 1953.

After disembarking from the *New Australia* at Pusan in South Korea, they travelled to Camp Casey, where they took part in a huge parade to commemorate the fact that the whole of the Australian Infantry was there: 1, 2 and 3RAR. This has never happened again outside Australia.

After some training and other duties, Frenchy Ray found himself in the real war. He and his partner, Kevin Tupper, were presented with an expensive 'Sniper Scope' infrared rifle. It had the ability to see in the dark, but needed a heavy car battery carried in a backpack to operate the sight. It was still on the secret list and they were warned not to let it fall into enemy hands.

Frenchy Ray with a Sniper Scope rifle.

As they were shown this impressive weapon, they realised there was no ammunition for it. There was an embarrassed silence when they pointed this out to the officer in charge.

> I was given a Jeep and a new slouch hat to go to the American line to swap the hat for carbine ammunition. We had no problem in obtaining a huge quantity of bullets which lasted us till the end of the war.

On their first night patrol with the 'Sniper Scope', Kevin Tupper accompanied Frenchy to cover him with an Owen gun. Leading the patrol, Frenchy would stop every minute or so to examine the ground ahead through his infrared scope.

> As the guys behind me could not see me, they only way they could stop was by colliding with the man in front. In no time, a good mortar bomb landing nearby would have collected the lot of us but that, at the time, was the least of my problems.

> Firstly I was scared, secondly I did not want to fall into a Chinese ambush, and thirdly I wasn't too happy at all the noise behind me: 'Shit, move up, you bastard, etc.'

> Some 300 or 400 yards from our line I came across some bushes which required some investigation. I froze. I could see some dark green men (infrared shows up green in the scope) holding black objects in their hand (obviously weapons).

> I kept on looking round to see how many enemy were in front of us, when the patrol commander pushed me in the ribs and said, 'Move on, we can't stay here all night,' to which I whispered in his ear, 'There are some gooks in front of us.'

The officer was eventually persuaded, and the patrol stayed put until shortly before daylight, when they returned to their own lines.

They took the 'Sniper Scope' out every second night because the battery had to be recharged as there was no spare, so during the day Frenchy and Kevin reverted to daylight sniping.

> On 12 May at the crack of dawn I left for no-man's land with my faithful 303 rifle. I advised the forward platoon of my time of return and marched down the hill. It's the time of day when ambushes are unlikely. One can see fairly clearly ahead in the early morning light.

> The area had been shelled so often that no trees could be seen, just a few sparse bushes covered the countryside. I organised myself for a day of sniping, laying under some bushes. After some hours of looking around I heard a rifle being fired some 200 yards in the west-front of me. My heart started to beat. At last I was close to a Chinese sniper.

I kept on looking for a long time but spotted nothing. This time when the Chinese fired his rifle once more, I saw a tiny puff of smoke filtering through a bush. I knew now where he was hiding but still could not see him through my telescope. I waited a fairly long time just watching the bush when I heard another crack of the rifle.

I lined up my rifle, nice and steady as if on the rifle range, and fired a single shot. Nothing happened, nothing moved. I waited another half hour and fired another shot. Still no move from the enemy.

I passed the rest of the day waiting for his next move. Nothing. I had only two options, I had either killed him or scared the daylight out of him. I was bursting for a smoke by this stage of the day, so I chewed a Camel cigarette from my C ration pack.

When it was time to move back, I started to worry that if I had missed 'Charlie' he might not miss me. Instead of boldly marching out, I crawled very slowly to the east, avoiding travelling the same way I had come.

Hot box meals arrive.

After a long crawl, I stood up behind a low ridge and marched briskly in the direction of our lines. Getting close to our forward trenches, I saw the dust of two bullets landing at my feet. I dived into a shell hole. I was fired on not by the Chinese but by our own troops.

I studied my map carefully, and came to the conclusion that I was a long way from my own line and was facing the Canadian position. I had drifted too far to the east. I poked my head above the rim of the shell hole and within a second a bullet crashed beside me. Thank God, who ever fired at me was a lousy shot, especially at such short range.

Knowing that the Canadians were mostly French speaking, I yelled in French, 'Ne tirez pas' while waving my hand above my head. I heard the reply, 'Avancez'. I took the plunge and jumped out of the shell hole and yelled that I was an Australian going in the wrong direction. A Canadian pointed out the right direction and called out 'bonne chance.'

After a spot of leave in Tokyo, Frenchy Ray's unit was sent to The Hook where they relieved a British unit. There the rival front lines were very close to each other and, with talk of an armistice to be signed at any time, orders were given to company commanders to avoid Australian casualties. The men were not told this in order to prevent demoralisation.

Meanwhile, the fighting continued. Frenchy and Kevin found themselves a bunker inside a tunnel from which to carry out their sniping.

The bunker has been the site of a lot of fighting judging by the number of dead Chinese around it. The head of a freshly decapitated Chinese was staring at us through the opening [a 'window' consisting of a wooden frame supported by sandbags].

We were told that all the forward troops would be on 'stand to' alert all night and every night. This was perfectly logical as all attacks started at night.

We could see the Chinese trenches about 200 yards [180 m] in front of us. On our left, we could see behind the Chinese trenches facing the US Marines on Hill 111. On the night of 13 July the Chinese started to attack.

We did not know it at the time but the Chinese did not intend to take The Hook. Such a prospect had been too costly for them in human terms with our deadly accurate artillery fire. They assumed we were numerically bigger than in reality.

At the time we had two companies in the front line, Charlie Company on the left and Baker Company on the right, probably around 300 men. The Chinese could be counted in thousands.

As the days dragged by there was still no sign of an armistice.

About 11 o'clock [on 23 July] two Chinese officers (we guessed because Chinese do not wear badges of rank in the field), one carrying a large pair of binoculars, the other with a map case, were both standing on top of the trench, right in front of us. What a beautiful target. Selecting one each, we fired simultaneously. They fell backwards in perfect unison. No other Chinese officers appeared for the rest of the day.

On 27 July, just after breakfast, the company was told to parade.

We were to leave only a skeleton crew to defend the place. To our ultimate surprise we were instructed by the CSM to leave our weapons guarded near the Company's command post to avoid shooting each other by accident.

[We were] addressed by the CSM who explained the terms of the truce and the ultimate details of the cease fire. Nobody leaped for joy or showed any great sign of satisfaction. It was not a surprise. The armistice had been negotiated for months.

The troops were told to avoid any incidents that might irritate the enemy and to start packing up. They had 72 hours to move 3 miles [4.8 km] from the front lines after destroying the bunkers, tunnel and weapon pits. The Chinese had to do the same, leaving a strip of six miles [9.6 km] empty of all troops to be called the Demilitarised Zone (DMZ). The truce would come into effect at 10 pm.

That day passed slowly. No one wanted to be the last casualty of the war. We were at the receiving end of some Chinese bombs but the whole front was rather calm. Presumably to get rid of an overload of ammunition, the Chinese started shelling our lines seriously as soon as it got dark, as well as firing all sorts of coloured flares in the sky.

At 10 pm all firing stopped. It was unreal. The whole front was quiet. We became aware of the complete silence. We could speak softly once more. It was rather eerie and strange and it was hard to get to sleep in such silence.

Few men from generation to generation are privileged to be witness to a historical event. We knew when we got up at 4 am that this day would be unique. The experience would remain engraved in our minds forever.

The valley in front was covered with a thick fog. We decided we would go and meet our enemies on the opposite trench. To show that we were friendly, we took off our tin hat and flak jacket. We were bare to the waist. In my case I decided to carry my large pair of binoculars.

Our faith in the Chinese was based only on the fact that they had stopped firing at the time stipulated. We hoped that they were good at keeping their word. We could hear Chinese music being played on loud speakers and as we got nearer we saw large flags of all colours lining the side of the Chinese trenches.

We walked slowly, not knowing what was going to happen. Suddenly we froze. Like a rabbit out of a hole, a Chinese appeared from an opening in the ground. We were about four feet from a smiling enemy.

He wore glasses and a green cap. To our complete amazement he said in perfect English, 'Good morning gentlemen. Have you had breakfast yet?' We were stunned and we mumbled 'Not yet.' 'Well, if you don't mind, gentlemen, can you please come back a little later whilst I have my breakfast?'

Frenchy recalls that he was told not to come in because of his binoculars.

They were taking me for a spy. Kevin and I sat on a rock and smoked a cigarette. After a while Kevin went to see if our Chinese was ready. I stayed relaxing on the rock.

Shaking hands with Chinese soldiers.

Just then a war correspondent arrived with a movie camera saying he was filming for the BBC. Frenchy advised him not to go into the Chinese trenches until the fog had completely cleared. As he sat on a rock, the cameraman knocked his camera, which fell into a bomb crater. As he moved to get it, Frenchy advised him that most bomb craters were either mined or booby-trapped in some way.

> I left him nearly in tears. I was thinking that I had missed an opportunity to be famous. In fact, no film was ever shown of the Australians meeting the Chinese on Armistice Day.

He moved a few yards and met three Chinese soldiers with whom he shook hands and exchanged cigarettes.

> At this stage, the number of Chinese soldiers had increased considerably and many Australian Diggers joined in. We saw little groups exchanging souvenirs, some showing photographs of their wives or girl friends.

> The vision of peace was marred by the extraordinary sight and smell of the thousands of rotten Chinese bodies laying all over the place. In the course of the afternoon the Chinese brought in a bulldozer to dig a large trench to be used as a mass grave. The bodies were brought in on stretchers and dropped over the side. When completely filled, the bulldozer pushed some earth on the top of the grave. No ceremony of any sort was carried out.

Supplied by Cyril 'Frenchy' Ray of Queensland

PREPARING FOR A
NICE EASY SHOOT

Flying Officer A R (Dick) Turner DFC
77 Squadron, Royal Australian Air Force
Korea 1950–1952

Dick Turner lied about his age to join the Army in 1942. He was only 16 and had told the recruiting officer he was two years older than that. He was serving in New Guinea when the truth was discovered. Of course he was sent home.

Two years later, at the age of 18, he joined the RAAF and travelled to Canada under the Empire Air Training Scheme where he eventually qualified as a pilot just as the war in Europe was ending.

Disappointed that he had not been able to contribute to the cause, he became a civilian but rejoined the RAAF in 1949 and served with 77 Squadron in Japan for almost 12 months before the Korean War started.

Dick Turner had two tours of duty with the RAAF, the first based in Japan flying Mustangs and the second based in Korea flying Meteor jet fighters. In all, he flew 244 sorties in a wide range of weather conditions and earned a Distinguished Flying Cross (DFC).

As he took part in so many missions, inevitably some were more memorable than others but Dick recalls one in particular, a raid on a railway tunnel, with some embarrassment.

> During a pilot's operational life, events occur which not only cause instant fear but trigger a mental response which, on later reflection, can only be described as crass stupidity.
>
> Being human, the tendency is to banish both the fear and the response into the deepest recesses of the mind, revealing them to no one, especially the 'stupidity' bit. Only after many years can the mind be persuaded to give up its darkest secrets to public scrutiny. In psychiatric circles it is known as the 'what the hell' syndrome.

Flying Officer Dick Turner with Meteor jet fighter.

During the early desperate days of the Korean War, we were carrying out a ground interdiction role from a PSP strip at Taegu, with the front line no more than five miles [8 km] away. The North Koreans were resupplying by train during the night, avoiding daylight air attacks by running the trains into the mountain tunnels until nightfall.

Our intelligence quickly became aware of this tactic and constant efforts were made to seal both ends of the tunnels, hopefully with the trains still inside. At a briefing on one such mission we were told that the expected enemy flak would be 'light to non-existent'.

Heartened by this, I confidently settled into my rocket dive, retrimmed the aircraft, put the 'pipper' on the tunnel entrance and prepared for a nice easy 'shoot'.

Suddenly the side of the mountain seemed to erupt . . . streams of tracer poured up . . . lazily at first, then with frightening rapidity, flicking over both wings and around the fuselage. All thoughts of an accurate strike disappeared (frightful admission), I was only concerned as to how the hell I was going to get out of this situation. Now comes the stupid part.

Although the flak was intensifying by the second, I had not been hit. Displaying a remarkable capacity for self-deception (based on illogical thinking) I convinced myself that I must be in some sort of 'safety cone' and all that was necessary to ensure my survival was to continue along the existing flight path, without deviation, and all would be well—so I did and it was. The principle of exquisite, masterly inactivity carried out to perfection.

Releasing my rocket load at approximately the right height, I hauled back on the stick, tightened the sphincter, slipped over the mountain top and headed for home— unscathed.

Over the years I have frequently thought about this mission and my feelings during it. I am grateful that the episode went largely unobserved, by people on our side anyway. Another set of eyes may have seen it differently—you know the sort of thing, 'complete disregard for own safety . . . relentlessly attacked the target through a storm of . . . ' etc, etc.

It would have been humiliating, having to say to the Monarch at the Investiture, 'I'm sorry, Ma'am, I cannot accept this . . . it didn't happen that way at all.'

Having read the above, you will readily understand my reluctance in bringing the matter forward. Never, in the whole history of aerial warfare has such a saga of poltroonery and irrational behaviour been brought to the attention of one's peers. I'll try to do better in the next war.

Whatever Dick Turner may have written about that particular incident, there was little doubt that on other occasions he knew exactly what he was doing. According to the official citation for his award of the DFC:

> On 6 September 1952, his squadron was called upon to attack a vitally important target, consisting of a dangerous build-up of enemy troops, in the North Eastern sector of Korea.
>
> Flying Officer Turner led this raid, and despite adverse weather conditions and intense, accurate anti-aircraft fire, brilliantly led the attack, and the squadron destroyed the target.

The citation went on to say that Flying Officer Turner had displayed courage and tenacity of the highest order.

Dick Turner recently returned to Korea as a member of a 50th anniversary commemorative mission that included representatives of all services that served in the Korean War.

Supplied by Dick Turner of Victoria

WAR CORRESPONDENTS
WITHOUT A WAR

John Grigsby
War correspondent
Malaya 1955

 t's a dangerous business for journalists covering wars, but when the war isn't a war but an anti-terrorist action, things can be even tougher.

In September 1955, John Grigsby, a widely experienced journalist on *The Age* in Melbourne, was among a group of five journalists and photographers nominated by their papers to be Accredited War Correspondents to accompany the 2nd Battalion, The Royal Australian Regiment (2RAR) to Malaya the following month. 2RAR was the first Australian battalion committed to the newly formed Commonwealth Strategic Reserve involving Australian, British and New Zealand forces.

John Grigsby was to represent *The Age*, the *Sydney Morning Herald*, which also provided a photographer, the *Brisbane Courier Mail*, the *Adelaide Advertiser* and the *Hobart Mercury*.

Communist terrorists, or CTs, were infiltrating Malaya's northern states as part of a campaign to overthrow the Malayan Government. 2RAR was sent to join the 28th Commonwealth Brigade already engaging the CTs. Malaya was still a British colony.

Led by the notorious Chen Ping, the CTs, mostly Malayan Chinese, attacked from across the Malaya–Thailand border and so were also called insurgents. Resplendent in army officers' uniforms with a large 'C' for correspondent on their caps and shoulder flashes on their shirts and safari jackets stating 'Accredited War Correspondent', the journalists were ready for the fray.

> At short notice we were called back to Army PR and told to bring our shirts and safari jackets with us. Our curiosity as to the reason why was soon answered. The Federal Government had ruled that the 2nd Battalion was not going to war but rather it

was going into an anti-terrorist action. Therefore we journalists could not be War Correspondents.

Sharp scissors were produced and the word 'War' was cut from our shoulder flashes. We were now just Accredited . . . Correspondents.

Upon its arrival on the troopship *Georgic* in Georgetown, on the island of Penang off the coast of northern Malaya, the battalion was quartered in the historic colonial Minden Barracks.

We correspondents just did not fit in. The essential military routines and restrictions were a constant irritation. Access to telephones, particularly for calls back to our news desks, were limited with the military having priority. And the clattering of our portable typewriters at night disturbed other officers in the adjacent thin-walled rooms.

The correspondents decided to move into the equally historic Eastern Oriental Hotel in Penang.

It was really something out of the past. It had big, comfortable rooms, elegant dining and bar facilities, to say nothing of daily room services and laundry, which made our life a lot easier. Access to the Cable and Wireless telegraph office and local and international telephone services meant we could file our copy at any time.

Soon afterwards a platoon of 2RAR was ordered out on a familiarisation patrol in a known terrorist area.

We correspondents, now in jungle green, accompanied them. This meant we were protected by two armed soldiers and were lodged in a fortified kampong or village where we whiled away the hours. I was quite at home in jungle greens having worn them while serving with the RAAF in the Pacific in WWII.

After a boring day hanging about the kampong, dining off army field rations and fruit bought at the kampong stalls and smoking innumerable cigarettes, we were at last called to rejoin the platoon for transport back to Minden Barracks.

After a briefing by the intelligence officer and supervised interviews with some of the troops, we were at last able to file stories of at least some action by the troops. Up till then, we'd been able to send back only stories about troops settling into Minden, shopping in Georgetown or doing tourist things on leave.

Although the troops had not had any contact with CTs, the stories told of troops patrolling in oppressive jungle heat, sudden tropical downpours, snakes, scorpions, huge mosquitoes and tension and frustration (or relief) at not locating the enemy.

After nearly a month of waiting around fortified villages or elsewhere in the jungles, well behind patrols and with no sighting of any terrorists, the correspondents decided they would be better off waiting in Georgetown for the return of the patrols, which were now away for several days at a time.

> We were able to interview villagers who had experienced CT raids, local officials who had been harassed and rubber tappers who went out into the plantations each day with exactly enough food for one meal to reduce opportunities for CTs to get food supplies. These and other stories provided Australian newspaper readers with a good picture of what the CT insurgency was doing to the people of Malaya.

After about five weeks the correspondents' group broke up. From the Australian reader's point of view, the news value of the patrols and CT attacks was declining. One correspondent and one photographer went home. Another decided to stay a few more weeks, while John Grigsby and Hugh Clunies Ross, the photographer with the *Sydney Morning Herald*, set off to work their way down the Malay Peninsula to Singapore, looking for stories of interest to Australians.

They interviewed British unit commanders on their CT operations and took photographs of them. In Kuala Lumpur they interviewed Malaya's Chief Minister, Tenku Abdul Rahman, on Malaya's struggle for Merdeka (independence) and the killings and intimidation of and acts of terrorism against the Malayan people by the CTs.

In Singapore, John Grigsby and Hugh Clunies Ross spent a week with the RAAF's No 1 Squadron, which was flying Lincolns, and flew with them on bombing raids on CT hideouts and their jungle communication trails.

> This was a case of deja vu for me. During WWII, I was posted to No 2 Medium Bomber Squadron carrying out raids on Japanese forces, operating out of Hughesfield air base near Darwin.

After nearly three months, John Grigsby reported to his paper that 2RAR was now operating very close to the Thai border and was away for weeks at a time. Despite the fact the battalion was suffering some casualties, he could see no point in going back to Penang. The wire services were now covering the actions. He was told to come home.

John Grigsby says one of his greatest 'achievements' during his stint in Malaya was gaining supplies of Australian beer for 2RAR. His story and pictures of the troops longing for a cold Aussie beer, were widely published. The Swan brewery responded quickly with crates of cans on a ship sailing direct to Malaya. Other breweries soon followed. The Malayan beer was not to the taste of the Australian troops and was never cold enough.

> I returned home from an area where civilians and soldiers were being killed and wounded, where British and Australian ground forces engaged in torrid fire fights with the CT and the RAF and RAAF pounded them from the air. I am still wondering why I wasn't a 'war' correspondent.

Supplied by John Grigsby of the ACT

MINESWEEPER PATROLS DURING INDONESIAN CONFRONTATION

Tactical Operator Alan Smoothy
HMAS *Snipe,* Royal Australian Navy
Malaysia and Borneo 1965–1966

 Friction between Indonesia and the newly created state of Malaysia forced the Commonwealth Government to come out in support of Malaysia in 1953.

On 25 September, the Prime Minister, Robert Menzies, told the House of Representatives that any 'armed invasion or subversive activity, supported, directed or inspired from outside Malaysia', would mean Australia adding its military assistance to the efforts of Malaysia and the United Kingdom in the defence of Malaysia's territory, integrity and political independence.

Despite this action, Indonesia continued its campaign of attacks across the border and Australian troops from the 3rd Battalion, Royal Australian Regiment (3RAR) became involved for the first time against a group of infiltrators who landed from the sea at the mouth of the Kesang River.

Australian naval operations in Malaysia were increased to counter the threat of seaborne infiltration and HMAS *Yarra* and HMAS *Parramatta* became engaged in intercepting fast patrol boats and submarines.

The coastal minesweepers HMA Ships *Hawke*, *Snipe*, *Gulf* and *Curlew* began to patrol off the coast of Borneo, Malaysia and Singapore and were joined later by HMA Ships *Ibis* and *Teal*.

Alan Smoothy served on *Snipe* during 1965–1966, taking part in patrols, the searching of suspect boats, including fishing boats, and minesweeping duties.

Alan Smoothy in Hong Kong.

Snipe, along with other minesweepers, picked up several contacts on radar which we suspected were Indonesian. These boats were small, canoe-like with large outboard motors and very fast.

After firing several rocket flares and pursuing these boats for quite a while, we were successful in turning them back.

There was a curfew on boats operating after 6 pm.

During patrols off the coast of Malaysia and Borneo, we would pick up several contacts on radar. On picking up contact we went into action stations and proceeded to close the contact.

We carried a Malayan interpreter who called out for the boats to stop. If they didn't we would open fire with the flag deck mounted Bren gun, always over their heads.

This always had the required result. We then brought the boat alongside where an armed boarding party would carry out a search.

Alan Smoothy with Bren gun.

But things didn't always go according to plan.

One night we picked up a contact on radar and, after they failed to stop as requested by the interpreter, we opened fire with the Vickers machine gun, which was mounted in the bow.

We discovered that it was, in fact, a prize crew from another minesweeper, who were taking the boat back into harbour.

The following day the crew were returned to *Snipe* by the Malaysian police boat and we in turn took them back to HMAS *Ibis* the following day.

Supplied by Alan Smoothy of New South Wales

'WE WORKED AND LIVED
IN A KILLING ZONE'

Sergeant Brian Mayfield
Royal Australian Air Force
Vietnam 1968

Brian Mayfield was Orderly Room Sergeant and Secretary to the Commander RAAF Forces Vietnam (COMRAAFV) at RAAF Headquarters in Saigon throughout 1968. His tour of duty included the Tet and May offensives when North Vietnamese Army and Viet Cong troops attacked Saigon.

His office was in the Free World Building and he was billeted in the Plaza Hotel, generally travelling between the two buildings in an RAAF Kombi van. This was adapted by having the back seat facing the rear to provide additional firepower with weapons facing front and back.

Brian Mayfield recalls that the threat of booby traps in the vehicle was a constant fear. While at the Free World Building, it was parked in the compound but at night it had to be parked in the street as close as they could get to their accommodation.

Each morning they would carefully check for booby traps including devices placed in the petrol tank. When a request sent back to Support Command in Australia for a locking petrol cap was refused because 'they were not entitled to one', an enraged Air Commodore let them know what he thought of their regulations.

Brian Mayfield recalls the Tet Offensive vividly.

> On the first morning of the Tet offensive we found the foyer of the Plaza filled with Americans, the front entrance secure and no traffic outside (usually chaotic at this time of the morning). The streets were empty and, although fighting was going on, we made it to the Free World Building without making contact with the enemy.

Sergeant Brian Mayfield with Sergeant Jim White outside
the Free World Building shortly before the Tet offensive.

As the day wore on and the sounds of fighting could be heard, our officers liaised with the Army over our situation. The inter-service rivalry came to the fore and Wing Commander Johnson told the Army we would defend our own area. At that point the building and surrounds were secured and we set up guard on full alert—meaning no sleep as we waited for a possible attack.

Over the following two to three days we waited, ate C rations and 'food' (amazing what can be made with bully beef) from the Army Field Kitchen set up in the compound and watched as the fighting increased all around us.

2 Squadron and 9 Squadron finally came to our assistance with weapons, ammunition, hand grenades, flak jackets and food. We felt we were then in a better position if the enemy attacked us. The Americans kept the compound lit up for us by dropping flares to light up the building and compound.

They kept guard from the roof of the building and from windows and other vantage points, ever vigilant for an enemy attack.

The area of Cholon directly in front of us and also to the north and south was subjected to attack by the South Vietnamese Skyraider aircraft. The population was warned to leave the area, which was then bombed in order to move the NVA and Viet Cong out.

Brian Mayfield said the May offensive came as no real surprise and they were better prepared. However, it also brought an increase in terrorist activities in the city and mortar and 122-mm rocket attacks became commonplace. These circumstances, coupled with the demands of their work, engendered intense stress.

The workload was very great. The pressure to perform was unrelenting and at times extreme. We worked and lived in a 'killing zone' with the advent of the Tet and May offensives of 1968 when we saw and experienced the onslaught of the North Vietnamese and Viet Cong.

The very fact that we were contained in the Free World Building for days with the fighting going on around us, that we had to wear flak jackets, arm ourselves and be at the ready with loaded weapons whenever we left the building, not knowing whether we would be ambushed or had to defend ourselves against the unseen enemy that was amongst us had its effect on us all.

Having to check underneath our vehicles, carefully checking under the bonnet and then last but not least starting the engine and hoping that it was not booby-trapped. This daily ritual was necessary when the terrorist activities started.

Another difficult fact of everyday life was the indiscriminate firing of 122-mm rockets by the North Vietnamese and the Viet Cong into the city. Food was another problem.

> There was a lack of proper diet due to the inconsistencies of and limited food available at the American Bachelor Enlisted Quarters (BEQs) and the workloads sometimes precluded us getting to the BEQs before the dining rooms closed (particularly during 5 pm and 7 pm curfew).

What was worse than the unremitting stress of life in Saigon was the humiliation they felt at the contempt expressed by some fellow countrymen when they returned to Australia.

> I would not have missed the opportunity to go to Vietnam, but the experience changed me forever. Having to stand guard in empty streets (24 hour curfew) locked out, unable to move as it would have drawn friendly fire, listening to the scattered sounds of fire fights and waiting for the enemy which I would have had to kill or be killed, will be with me all the days of my life.

> We were not trained for the situation we found ourselves in, were led by officers who never briefed us properly at any time, and gave the impression they were there to get a 'gong'. Thankfully they never did.

> Vietnam will always be with me with the happy times (I met my wife there), sad times (the death and destruction around us) and above all how we as Australians must protect our precious democracy and freedom.

> I believe the Government of the time was wrong, our people humiliated us on our return, and it changed us forever. May it never happen again.

Brian Mayfield returned to Saigon in 1998 with his Vietnamese wife and his children. It was an intensely emotional time as he recalled the horrors of his wartime experiences while visiting the places in which he had lived and worked.

> When I took my children to the Free World Headquarters (now the Ky Hoa Hotel) I was overcome with emotion.

> The feeling was overwhelming and I cried and could do nothing about it. This was where we boarded ourselves up and waited for the enemy during the Tet offensive. The area was the scene of massive destruction and loss of life over those few critical days.

> Standing in the grounds with my children I think that my war finally ended with the outpouring of emotion.

Supplied by Brian Mayfield of New South Wales

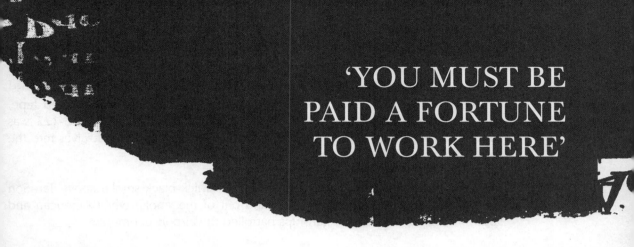

'YOU MUST BE PAID A FORTUNE TO WORK HERE'

Don Hook
War Correspondent
Indochina 1968–1970

Don Hook had more than 16 years experience as a journalist in Australia, Britain and Papua New Guinea before becoming an ABC News correspondent in South-East Asia in December 1967. He also had reasonable military experience as a school cadet, a National Serviceman, as an NCO in the Papua New Guinea Volunteer Rifles, and as a Reserve officer at PNG Command Headquarters.

On the eve of the February 1968 Tet offensive in Vietnam, I was in a RAF [Royal Air Force] Hercules flying to Singapore from Mauritius with cine-cameraman Neil Davis. We'd spent the previous week in Mauritius with British troops flown in from Malaysia to quell racial clashes between the island's Muslim and Creole communities.

About two hours out of Singapore, the captain of the Hercules called us onto the flight deck. An urgent message was being broadcast by the British Embassy in Saigon stating that a major attack on the city appeared to be underway.

When we landed at Singapore at 4 am there was a message from the ABC to pick up new film stock, batteries and other gear and head for Saigon as quickly as possible.

A quick check revealed that all commercial flights to Saigon were cancelled. Six hours and numerous telephone calls later we flew by commercial airline to Penang Island in north-west Malaysia and then took a taxi to the RAAF Base at Butterworth on the mainland. The news from Saigon was bad with fighting in and around the American Embassy.

The RAAF kindly gave us space on its regular C-130 [Hercules] supply flight to Vung Tau that left early the next morning. We were over Vietnam when we were told the aeroplane had been loaded incorrectly and we would have to land at Phanrang with supplies for the Australian Canberra squadron based there.

Don Hook records the announcement of the awarding
of the Victoria Cross to Warrant Officer Ray Simpson

It was 5 pm by the time we reached Vung Tau. RAAF officers told us that there were no more flights to Saigon that day and arranged transport to take us to their mess. We'd just loaded 13 boxes of ABC gear—it was in the days before video tape, satellite phones and transistors—when the tower advised that a Thai C-123 was about to take off for Saigon. We literally threw our luggage and ourselves into the aeroplane moments before it became airborne.

Miles out from Saigon we could see columns of thick black smoke above Tan Son Nhut airport. Fighter planes flashed in and out of the smoke while American and South Vietnamese helicopter gunships patrolled the airport perimeter.

With the back door open, we dived steeply for our landing, pulled up quickly and taxied to a high, horseshoe-shaped revetment where the cargo and passengers were unloaded. Within minutes, the Thais were on their way back to Vung Tau.

We remained in the sandbag revetment until after dark. There was an almost constant thud of incoming mortar shells while the sky above was full of flares and tracers, helicopter gunships, and modified Dakotas blaring out messages in Vietnamese as part of the psychological war against the Vietcong. It was two hours before transport arrived to take us to an American officers club on the southern perimeter of the huge airport.

A short time later a mortar shell flattened the nearby chapel in which some recent arrivals had chosen to sleep. I never learned their fate. Welcome to Vietnam! Welcome to the war!

To work in Vietnam a correspondent required very little; a letter from one's employer and a valid passport—that was about it. One became accredited to the United States Military Assistance Command Vietnam (MACV). This entitled one to full co-operation and assistance, within the bounds of operational requirements and military security. In other words, one could obtain a uniform, rations and quarters and move about Vietnam using air, water and ground transportation.

Correspondents received a US Department of Defense noncombatant's certificate of identity, a detailed identity card that was supposed to be useful if one were captured by the Vietcong/NVA [North Vietnamese Army]. No one believed it would be useful; some thought the opposite would be the case. But the card was handy, along with one's MACV card, in moving around the country with the Army of the Republic of Vietnam (ARVN), and was accepted by the Australian, New Zealand, Thai and Republic of Korea (ROK) forces, as well as 'Free World' aid agencies. At times, it was also handy in Cambodia and Laos, although both countries issued their own accreditation documents.

One of the difficulties facing a newly arrived correspondent was the military jargon, the acronyms, abbreviations, contractions and other verbal shorthand in wide and constant use. One had to become used to KIA (later KHA), WIA, MIA, DMZ, LZ, BDA, CA, BEQ, BOQ and terms such as hot insert, incoming, organic weapon and third world national.

In 1968 the number of foreign correspondents covering the Vietnam War peaked at 650, roughly the equivalent of an infantry battalion. The Americans allocated the equivalent of two battalions to look after them. It's interesting to note that only 27 reporters went ashore with the first wave at Normandy on D-Day 1944; almost 50 years later some 2500 covered Desert Storm.

1968 was a bad year for the Americans as the number of US troops killed each month rose from 300 to 500. Television footage of the Tet offensive had a profound effect on the morale of the American people. These and other factors led to international condemnation of the war. The so-called My Lai massacre, involving troops of the Americal Division, also took place in 1968. It was a bad year too for correspondents. Several died in helicopter crashes and a number were killed, including three Australians and a British colleague, in an ambush in Cholon on May 5.

The time zone was kind to Australian correspondents in Vietnam; there was only one hour's difference between Saigon and eastern Australia. For the Americans it was not so convenient; most had deadlines either late at night or early morning.

As an ABC correspondent in Saigon, my day began about 5 am by checking with American and ARVN 'briefers' (briefing officers) on overnight activities. This often provided stories for the ABC main breakfast/morning news and current affairs bulletins as well as for Radio Australia, which, in those days, operated 24 hours a day.

The remainder of the morning and early afternoon was taken up with developing earlier stories, interviews with military and political people, occasional visits to the Australian Embassy and Australian military headquarters, planning trips outside Saigon, office administration, and shipping film and tapes to Australia or to the ABC's Asian Office in Singapore.

About 4 o'clock there was the ARVN daily briefing, which usually made extravagant claims about Vietcong/NVA losses, followed by the American briefing ('The Five o'clock Follies'), which made even more extravagant claims about Vietcong/NVA losses.

The American 'briefers' were smartly turned out officers, mostly of major rank, who usually had served at least one tour of duty in the field.

In the main, they were articulate, experienced, knowledgeable and popular with the correspondents although they freely admitted that 'some people are called to die for their country, while others are called to lie for their country'.

It was usually nine o'clock and well past the 6 pm curfew by the time I'd checked out facts and figures, written my stories, and filed them through the Reuters office.

In the field we did what the military did, apart from actually fighting. We carried a lot of broadcasting equipment in addition to water, rations and our personal gear. As non-combatant correspondents, we were not supposed to carry weapons and ammunition although we were often asked to do so. I didn't carry weapons but I knew correspondents who did . . . and I knew some who used them.

The relationship with troops in the field was usually very good. I was often asked if I had to be in Vietnam. I'd reply, 'Not really.' I explained that I'd applied for a posting to south-east Asia with the ABC and Indo-China was part of the region. However, I could—if I so desired—return to Australia at any time. I remember one soldier shaking his head and saying to me, 'Man, you are crazy. If I could go home now, I would. You must be crazy.' Others often asked questions related to my pay. 'You must be paid a fortune to work here,' they'd say. I'd tell them I wasn't (which was true) but they didn't seem to believe me. They'd just say things like 'bullshit, mate' or 'tell us another'.

In the main I found it was much easier to get the story than to get it back to Australia. Written copy usually was sent through Reuters and that was quite reliable. The big problem was with voice and film reports. It was often impossible to get a phone line or broadcast circuit through to Australia. Sometimes I sent voice reports to the BBC in London and they were passed on to the ABC. On other occasions, such as when the transmitters were damaged during the Tet and May offensives, I sent reports on the Voice of America circuit to New York. They were passed to the ABC's correspondent in Washington who sent them to Radio Australia in Melbourne, who in turn sent them to ABC News in Sydney.

Apart from the military, correspondents found good contacts among the foreign diplomats, businessmen, French and Vietnamese journalists, aid workers, missionaries and Saigon government officials. I also received a good deal of background information from members of the International Control Commission that was made up of representatives from India, Poland and Canada. At one stage I lived next door to an Indian Army signals officer; he was the source of several good stories as well as providing quick information on currency fluctuations.

The Vietnam War was 'uncensored' in the sense that media people could move virtually anywhere they wanted and there was no outward censorship of stories, photographs, tapes or film. There were, of course, certain ground rules under which correspondents could not report on matters which might place operations in jeopardy.

It was a different story in Cambodia where outgoing stories had to be lodged with the censor's office. Correspondents soon learned to get around the censor, either by flying out to Bangkok with their stories, tapes and film or by having them carried out of the country by airline passengers.

During the early days of the Lon Nol takeover of Cambodia in 1970, several correspondents were killed as a result of poor military briefings. The aptly named Major Am Rong sent at least two of my colleagues to their death down the infamous Highway One, having assured them that the route was safe and under the control of Lon Nol forces.

There were also tragic misunderstandings with ARVN and US forces. A Reuters correspondent and I accompanied Lon Nol forces when they recaptured the riverside university town of Kampong Cham. The Khmer Rouge force was quickly driven out with only a handful of Lon Nol casualties. Minutes later, low-flying ARVN T-28s began strafing us, killing some 60 troops and wounding dozens more. For the first time in Indo-China, I thought that I, too, was about to die. Until then, I hadn't really considered that possibility; I was quite detached from it.

One of the great characters among the correspondents in Vietnam was the British journalist Donald Wise, a World War II infantry officer who was wounded and later captured by the Japanese in Singapore in 1942.

Wise liked Australians, possibly because of the Diggers he met in the POW camps; Australians certainly liked him.

One had to spend only a short time with two of his Aussie mates—the irrepressible Francis Patrick 'Pat' Burgess and Visnews cameraman Neil Davis—and one would be splitting one's side laughing at stories involving Don Wise. Sadly, all three are now dead. Davis was killed covering a Thai military coup in 1985; Burgess died in Sydney and Wise in England, both in the 1990s.

Burgess and Wise were the most unlikely friends. Cambridge-educated Donald, a tall man with a bristling David Niven-style moustache and erect bearing, was very much the pukka Englishman abroad—dashing and dapper in his well-tailored tropical clothing. Pat, an Irish-Australian born at Warwick, Queensland, on St Patrick's Day 1927, was big and noisy. Almost as tall as Wise, he was the bronzed Anzac, the Bondi lifesaver and the street-wise Sydney larrikin rolled into one. And as for clothing, it was usually Australian or American military fatigues; occasionally he would dress up in a well-worn correspondent's safari suit.

One of Pat's (and my) favourite stories was about their visit to the first Australian infantry battalion to arrive in Vietnam. Donald was wearing a tailored Tiger suit of the (South) Vietnamese Marines when they arrived at the Bien Hoa base. Two Diggers were on guard at the entrance. One turned to the other and, cocking his thumb at Donald, said, 'Geez mate, we're saved. Bloody Tarzan's joined us.'

Wise later told colleagues that he met the Australian battalion commander and was flown by helicopter to a forward position. The CSM [Company Sergeant-Major] took him to a bunker and, as evening approached, found him a stretcher, mosquito net, and rations. 'He did everything apart from tucking me into bed and kissing me goodnight.'

Wise said that given his treatment, he could not believe reports that the Australians were anti-media and disliked journalists.

At dawn the next morning as the Australian troops were moving off on patrol, he heard the CSM being questioned by a young officer.

'Did you make Mr Wise comfortable and welcome?'

'Yes sir. We put him right out with the point platoon . . . like we do with all those bloody journalists.'

Neil Davis and Wise made outrageous bets with each other as well as sharing a liking for 'black' or sick humour. Tim Bowden, in his book *One Crowded Hour*, suggests this diverted them from the horrors that shattered other people.

Davis had a long-standing bet with Wise that he [Wise] would be killed before Davis. It was one of the few bets Neil lost.

Supplied by Don Hook of the ACT

'VIETNAM'S ROLLS ROYCE DEALER, 106 FIELD WORKSHOP'

Major Claude Palmer
106 Field Workshop
Royal Australian Electrical and Mechanical Engineers
Vietnam 1969–1970

U nits of the Royal Australian Electrical and Mechanical Engineers (RAEME) have served Australia well in many conflicts and Vietnam was no exception. Their skill and dedication to keeping essential equipment repaired and in good working order are well recognised.

106 Field Workshop was one of the few Australian units to be raised in a theatre of war. From 1969 to 1970 Major Claude Palmer was Officer-in-Charge of the unit. He recalled that while the first priority in Vietnam was fighting the war, an essential element of Australian operations was the winning of the hearts and minds of the local Vietnamese.

> Since the earliest deployment in the Sudan, the Australian Digger has always opened his heart and his wallet to the local children—especially those disadvantaged by war.

> So members of 106 Field Workshop readily adopted the Ba Ria Orphanage and, later, the Long Tan primary school. There were regular runs with 'surplus' rations, sweets, building repairs, well cleaning, and even playground equipment.

The local people gratefully acknowledged these activities. At Christmas 1969, Major Palmer received a card from the local school: 'Dear Major, We, All the teachers, wish you, the benefactors of our school, A MERRY CHRISTMAS and A HAPPY NEW YEAR signed Representative Nguyen van Huy.'

106 Field Workshop was extremely proud of its work in the field. It not only repaired damaged vehicles such as tanks and Armoured Personnel Carriers (APCs), often under extreme conditions, but it also worked on making improvements to existing equipment.

Members of a 106 Field Workshop patrol in 1969.

So many casualties occurred as a result of vehicles hitting mines that 106 Field Workshop was asked to design and construct armour kits, and after a number of trials using VC [Viet Cong] mines and damaged APCs, a design was approved. This additional armour became a universal modification for Australian APCs and proved so effective that it saved many young soldiers from death or serious injuries.

Claude Palmer was later a member of the Duntroon Entry Selection Board and once in 1977 the Board convened in Sydney and had accommodation in Kings Cross. The meeting had adjourned and the members were walking to dinner along Darlinghurst Road, near the famous El Alamein fountain, when a young man rushed up to Claude. 'I know you—your unit designed that anti-mine kit that was fitted to my APC in Vietnam,' he said. He then shook Claude's hand firmly, saying, 'I've wanted to thank you personally for years. Soon after your boys rearmoured my APC, it hit a mine. Thanks to your work, my mates and I survived in one piece.'

On one occasion, a Centurion tank was badly damaged when it struck a Viet Cong mine during clearing operations near Nui Dat. It was essential that it be back in operation as soon as possible. Following closely behind the tank were members of 106 Field Workshop, travelling in their specially adapted armoured mobile repair unit. The tank's track assembly was a complete write-off but the team still managed to repair it, replacing the complete front suspension unit, front idler wheels and track in only eight hours.

There was intense but friendly rivalry between the various units and this manifested itself in many ways.

> The Centurion tank being used by the Australian Army was powered by a V 12 petrol engine originally designed and built by Rolls Royce for the Spitfire fighter aircraft. Tanks repaired by 106 were adorned by a stencil which read: 'Serviced exclusively by Vietnam's Rolls Royce dealer, 106 Field Workshop'. Not to be outdone, the APC Repair Section somehow obtained Detroit Diesel insignias and attached them to their overalls. (The M113A1 APC had a Detroit Diesel engine matched to an Allison transmission.)

> Australian soldiers are famous for a strong sense of humour under the most arduous conditions. The Task Force rubbish dump some 500 metres distant received much daily traffic. The local VC observed this, and, logically but wrongly, assumed that the Headquarters must be there, and so launched a rocket attack at what they thought must be a prime target. When it became apparent that 106 was not the target, 106 soldiers within sight of the dump could be heard cheering at each impact, rather like a crowd at a darts game.

> Officially unacknowledged though it may be, Diggers of the first and second AIF were known to creatively interpret regulations to achieve what had to be achieved. Following in the great tradition, men of 106 did likewise, and to this day, no one has

revealed the true identity of a certain Sergeant E Kelly whose signature appeared on certain requisitions at the US Depot at Long Binh.

Resourceful 106 craftsmen would often scrounge unserviceable equipment that had been rejected by the US Army from salvage dumps, and repair it to operational use, thus saving the Australian taxpayer many thousands of dollars.

Claude was full of praise for the work of voluntary organisations such as the Salvation Army.

Australian forces are fortunate in always having the Salvation Army and/or Everyman Organisation representatives. These courageous philanthropic souls provide welfare and spiritual advice, cold drinks, hot beverages, and biscuits to troops in action— sometimes literally. The local 'Sally' as he was affectionately known, had a rather battered Land Rover. When he was due to return to Australia for his well-earned week of R&R, he asked if 106 could perform an oil change on his vehicle while he was away. The men of the vehicle and general engineering platoons voluntarily completely rebuilt and repainted the vehicle so well that when he returned, he could not recognise his Land Rover which was waiting for him at the airstrip.

The unit adopted its own mascot, a young monkey known as Charlie Goloski. He spent much of his 'working' day in Recovery Platoon and would often go on recovery missions. He developed a taste for certain beverages and in the evenings was seen to swoop from the rigging of the mess tent to swipe an unattended can of beer, which he proceeded to drink.

Charlie Goloski met an untimely end when he discovered a bottle of sleeping tablets, which he promptly opened and ate. Despite desperate efforts from a US Army vet, Charlie never recovered. Later, another monkey, a female known as Suzie Goloski, replaced him. She remained with the unit until it returned to Australia, at which time she was given to the children of the Ba Ria Orphanage.

Supplied by Claude Palmer of Queensland

'THE MOST INTENSIVE AND EXCITING PERIOD'

Lieutenant Anthony McWatters
Australian Army attached to
4th Armoured Brigade, 1st Armoured Division, British Army
Operations Desert Shield and Desert Storm
Kuwait, Iraq 1991

I n 1989 and 1990, Lieutenant Anthony McWatters of the Australian Army was on a training posting with the British Army in Germany. He then went on active service on Operations Desert Shield and Desert Storm in the 1990–1991 Gulf War.

As a member of the 11th Armoured Workshop and 4th Armoured Brigade of the 1st British Armoured Division, British Army, he served in Saudi Arabia, Iraq and Kuwait leading up to and during the ground war that liberated Kuwait from Iraqi occupation. Anthony McWatters is currently serving at Oakey, Queensland.

Lieutenant McWatters kept extensive notes during his tour of duty in the Gulf. The original version of this article was written for a professional military audience immediately afterwards.

I was offered an appointment as second in command of an Armoured Workshop Forward Repair Group (FRG) recently warned for deployment as part of Operation Granby. I took up the post on 1 December 1990 with only three weeks to go before scheduled return to Australia from a 14-month aeronautical engineering training posting with the British Army in the UK and Germany. My wife, Elizabeth, and our two young children, Emily and Thomas, quickly adapted to the situation and decided to remain in Germany until my return from the Middle East. They were settled into the British Army community there and we knew they would be looked after by the extensive family support organisations that were quickly set up by the Army. The community spirit and comradeship was strong as the whole of the British Army of the Rhine was working very hard at getting the best possible force to the Gulf.

Lieutenant Anthony McWatters and Captain Mark Munday.

The 11 Armoured Workshop REME [Royal Electrical and Mechanical Engineers] was based at Soest in the Federal Republic of Germany in the north-west of the country. The unit was detached from the 3rd (UK) Armoured Division and placed under command of 1st (UK) Armoured Division for Operation Granby. Main Repair Group (MRG) 11 with two other MRGs was to be tasked and employed as a divisional asset. FRG 6 was placed under command of 4th Armoured Brigade as an independent sub unit and grouped with the Brigade Admin Area (BAA) units. The role was to provide second line repair and recovery support to the brigade. The priority was the Challenger tanks and Warrior Infantry Fighting Vehicles of the brigade's battle groups that were to be formed for operations predominantly from the following units:

- 14th/20th Regiment The Kings Hussars—(Challenger Tank Regiment)

- 1st Battalion The Royal Scots Regiment—(Warrior Armoured Infantry Battalion)

- 3rd Battalion The Royal Regiment of Fusiliers—(Warrior Armoured Infantry Battalion)

The FRG main body flew from Hanover on a chartered Tristar airliner into Dahran, Saudi Arabia, on 6 January 1991. A 100-km bus trip in old double deckers with singing Arab drivers, put us in the Al Jubail port area (Force Maintenance Area) at about 0200 hours the next morning.

Administration and registration in theatre with field records office took an hour or so and then it was off to Black Adder Camp, a tented staging camp on the outskirts. Acclimatisation, training, administration and meeting the equipment at the docks, were now the priorities.

Setting up liaison with headquarters and units, as well as getting to know the personalities at Divisional and Brigade HQs, was important. The 4th Armoured Brigade was already exercising in the desert so the pressure was on to get FRG 6 out to support the training.

The scale of the military build up was staggering. Every type of military hardware imaginable was being moved through the port area. Some entrepreneurial members of the unit soon had us supplied with some of the niceties of the American supply system through the 'swap' program. The famous US 'camp cot' stretchers were well sought after. An Australian Army slouch hat was worth nearly anything you wanted!

On 13 January, the FRG deployed 100 km north to Devil Dog Dragoon Range and training area to begin supporting the battle groups firing, battle runs and brigade exercise—of course it rained heavily that day!

The next two weeks were spent at a hectic pace in the training area. Being near to the coast, there were many areas of soft *sabkah* (low crusty salt pans) and the recovery crews were kept extremely busy extricating vehicles from severe bog situations. Power packs, engines, major assembly and electronic and optical equipment failures kept Forward Repair Teams (FRT) and optronics section heavily tasked around the clock.

When the Allied air offensive started on 17 January, it was initially a case of NBC (nuclear, biological and chemical) suits on/NBC suits off! Chemical agent warning and reporting procedures were sorted out after the initial first nerves and the training and tasking continued. The Iraqi Scud-B missiles were aimed at Al Jubail, Dahran and Riyadh over 100 km to the south and so had little effect on our day-to-day activities in 4th Armoured Brigade.

On 26 January, 4th Armoured Brigade moved north to Divisional concentration area Keyes about 60 km south of the Saudi/Kuwait border and east of the Wadi Al Batin. A new phase of training and preparations was conducted from Keyes. Two divisional exercises/rehearsals were conducted and plans for the final ground offensive against the Iraqi forces were developed.

Tactical exercises without troops and command post exercises at divisional level formed part of this planning and training. Activities in and from Keyes also served as part of an extensive deception plan; although at the time we knew nothing of that.

On 14 February, the division began a rehearsal and movement exercise advancing some 120 km to arrive, three days later, in concentration area Ray to the west of Keyes and some 60 km to the south of the Saudi/Iraq border to the west of the Wadi Al Batin. Things were getting much slicker now.

The serious problems of mass confusion encountered in the earlier exercises, particularly in the obstacle breach phases, were being ironed out. Everyone was a lot more confident. In FRG 6, FRT and recovery crew commanders were now proficient in independent desert navigation and operating with the battle groups of the brigade. Personalities throughout the organisation had learnt to work as a team. Final training and preparations were conducted in Ray and battle procedure carried out. Of course this didn't mean too much of a break for any REME soldier as the equipment had to be in the best possible condition for the coming operation.

G Day was 24 February 1991. The 1st US Infantry Division crossed into Iraq with air and artillery support from the British. Lanes were cleared through the Iraqi defences and an area secured to the north of the minefield/obstacle areas.

The concept for the British operation was a move through the breach lanes, passage of lines through the US positions and then attack objectives in Iraq and Kuwait as allocated. A reconstitution phase was planned and prepared for after the initial battles with subsequent operations as required. REME workload in the reconstitution was expected to be high.

A lot of work was done and resources allocated at corps and divisional level to anticipate and be ready for the reorganisation and regeneration that would be rapidly required before subsequent combat operations. Little used words like reclamation, salvage, battlefield clearance and equipment denial/destruction became the everyday reality for many of the REME members of 1 (UK) Armoured Division as they prepared for the ground war.

Immediately prior to crossing the breach into Iraq, FRG 6 detached some elements (FRT and recovery ARRVs [Armoured Repair and Recovery Vehicles]) to battle groups for the first phase and some further ARRVs were detached to provide brigaded recovery support to the breach operation.

Equipment casualties were recovered forward to designated Equipment Collection Point (ECP) grid references where inspection and repair (if appropriate) was effected. The initial successes of 4 Brigade and its rapid advance into Iraq from objective to objective meant a constant change in situation for the FRG.

The longest period in an ECP was approximately six hours so tasks such as power pack or final drive replacement had to be quick. Some resupply of major assemblies and power packs to FRG 6 was conducted by Royal Air Force Chinook and Royal Navy Sea King helicopters. Support helicopters proved their worth to the land forces in many ways during the conflict.

After the first objectives were achieved, detached elements returned to the FRG. Movement during the advance was from ECP to ECP independent of the BAA; at times well forward of BAA and others well behind. This independent movement across the battlefield was not carried out without problems and inadvertent involvement in combat actions.

Communications with brigade HQ were not always reliable and information on routes and by-passed enemy positions was unclear. Huge groups of prisoners guarded by one or two men with small arms (and sometimes unguarded) on occasion decided 'why not go back to our trenches and weapons'. Small arms and support weapon fire was common well behind the fighting echelons and FRG 6 was involved in some incidents.

Crews of disabled British tanks and AFVs [Armoured Fighting Vehicles] being towed behind ARRVs were extremely keen to get into the battle again and on more than one occasion, fired at targets of opportunity while under tow! Mines and unexploded bomblets were a constant hazard, especially at night or during sandstorms or rain (both of which were prevalent). Severe damage was caused to many vehicles when they struck some of these hazards. FRG members were involved in POW handling and administering first-aid to the wounded.

The clear priority from the brigade perspective was to ensure FRG 6 was keeping up with the battle groups and recovering equipment casualties forward. ECPs tended to be on or near recently cleared enemy positions, which added another dimension to the adventure. The men took every available opportunity to explore and gather souvenirs. This practice was dangerous and many soldiers were lucky, and shocked, at what they found.

The advance turned eastward towards Kuwait. Intelligence and situation reports were occasional but everyone knew that things were going far better than anyone had anticipated. On 27 February the advance halted for a few hours before the final advance into Kuwait was ordered.

This became a rapid charge towards Kuwait City. FRG 6 moved ahead of the BAA establishing ECPs and sweeping the route for equipment casualties about the axis of advance. Late on the night of 28 February, orders regarding the cease-fire were received. FRG 6 moved into the BAA about 30 km to the north-west of Kuwait City. That night and the next day the entire British Division moved through to establish itself to the north and west of the city.

Destroyed Iraqi tank and equipment.

That evening most grabbed their first real sleep for four days and were thankful things had gone so well. FRG 6 had sustained no personnel casualties and the most intensive and exciting period in just about everyone's life had finished. The carnage and destruction dealt to the Iraqis was sobering.

In our brigade two Warrior AFVs from 3rd Battalion the Royal Regiment of Fusiliers had been hit by friendly air attack resulting in nine fatalities. There were many other fatalities, wounds and close calls in British and all coalition force formations but they were small in number compared to the destruction dealt to the enemy.

FRG 6 had established 16 ECPs since arriving in Saudi Arabia and had completed in the vicinity of 130 power pack/engine replacements, 60 major assembly replacements and 54 logged recovery tasks. Now they were in Kuwait and there was more to follow!

4th Armoured Brigade was now adopting a defensive posture awaiting further developments. Priority was given to getting brigade equipment back up to pre-operational condition. It seemed that everyone was so happy about the success of the operation that they ignored the state of their equipment for a while. Slowly FRT workload increased again. As the days went by the possibility of a permanent cease-fire became reality and preparations for redeployment to Germany were begun.

An expedition back to Iraq and western Kuwait was arranged to clear the battlefield of useable military hardware. Brigades were responsible for their own areas and recovered equipment was eventually pooled under divisional control. Battlefield clearance is a hazardous and disturbing undertaking and one which, for practical reasons, is not often practised well during peacetime training exercises.

For the next three weeks the men of FRG 6 (and most other REME units in the division) had a constant job towing, dragging, repairing and driving enemy equipment. All varieties of serviceable Soviet, Chinese and European hardware including tanks, APCs [Armoured Personnel Carriers], artillery pieces and air defence weapons, vehicles and plant equipment were collected. Small arms and support weapons collected by individuals during and after the conflict had to be surrendered.

Teams of Royal Engineers and REME were formed to ensure that all equipment was safe prior to recovery. Booby traps were encountered in some areas and the sights and smells of the desert battlefield will remain vivid in the memories of the soldiers who participated, for the rest of their lives.

Enemy Equipment Collection Points (EECP) were established and grew into massive 'boneyards'. Only undamaged equipment was recovered. The majority had been destroyed during the war and no doubt still litters the desert. The novelty of playing with such an assortment of equipment quickly wore off and many a recovery mechanic was observed tearing his hair out when a T55 tank crashed into the back of his ARRV because rigid towing bars would not fit and chains were the only method of towing.

Serviceable captured vehicles were commissioned in many cases to supplement requirements in the post operation phase. A senior engineer acquired an air-conditioned Mercedes armoured command vehicle as his personal 'run-around' and Commander 4 Brigade posted two T55 tanks outside his headquarters as 'guards'. The intent was that all captured equipment would be recovered to Saudi Arabia but its eventual plight is unknown. Some units managed to ship 'war booty' trophies back to Germany or UK, but no doubt the majority is still in Kuwait or Saudi Arabia.

Having survived the Gulf War, Lieutenant McWatters was involved in a serious road accident in which four people, including himself, were injured and later admitted to a Norwegian Field Medical Hospital. One Land Rover and an 8-ton fuel truck were destroyed and two other trucks damaged.

Probably the biggest single killer throughout the war period, as usual, was road accidents. We were lucky to get away with it. I am ever grateful to the British and US Army fire and crash rescue experts who kept me breathing and extricated me alive from the wreckage of my Land Rover by adept and rapid winching, prying and cutting with some very handy crash rescue equipment.

The 11th Armoured Workshop REME was redeployed to Germany three months after it arrived in the Kuwait theatre of operations.

Supplied by Anthony McWatters of Queensland

'MAKING A CONTRIBUTION TO WORLD POLITICS'

Sergeant David Hartshorn
Multinational Force and Observers (MFO)
Sinai 1994

When Yasser Arafat made his first visit to the Sinai since his expulsion from the area in the 1960s, Sergeant David Hartshorn was on duty with the Australian contingent of the Multinational Force and Observers (MFO), known as Operation Mazurka.

The MFO was an international peacekeeping force in the Sinai to enforce the peace between Egypt and Israel.

Arafat arrived in his own aircraft on 1 July 1994 and was escorted through the UN base by the Australian commander of the MFO, Major General David Ferguson, and then headed off in a motorcade across the border to the Gaza Strip. There, he was greeted by tens of thousands of cheering Palestinians, according to a report in *Keesing's Record of World Events*.

Sergeant Hartshorn recalls that Arafat appeared to be 'quiet, quick witted and confident, but wary of anything that might go wrong.' He was accompanied by a strong contingent of bodyguards.

As the duty officer, Sergeant Hartshorn kept the Force Duty Centre log of the day's historical events. The log, map and situation reports on the visit are now with the Australian War Memorial.

In a letter to his family, Sergeant Hartshorn described the daily conditions.

> There is a relaxed professionalism here. The feeling you are doing something you have been trained for and are making a contribution to world politics.

Sergeant David Hartshorn receives his Active Service Medal for his time in Sinai from Bill Hayden.

A couple of days ago the force commander was driving back to camp and his driver saw an Israeli vehicle on fire. They stopped and rendered assistance by using the fire extinguisher in the commander's car as the Israelis don't have fire equipment in their vehicles.

Later on people were concerned about the commander stopping as it could have been a set up. It fortunately wasn't but even though we are sanctioned by both Egypt and Israel, there are people on both sides who don't want us here.

The Arafat visit was a highlight of his time in Sinai, but there were plenty of other interesting events to keep him busy. The MFO's force duty office received regular reports of incidents that required attention—often these were violations of access restrictions by heavily armed Bedouin.

A huge number of mines had been laid in the area and often injured or killed people who walked on them. Keeping track of the mines was almost impossible in the shifting desert sands.

On one occasion, Sergeant Hartshorn had to deploy members of the MFO who tried in vain to rescue two Egyptians who had fallen into a well they had been digging.

We commenced a 36-hour digging operation at the site but failed to recover the bodies. Due to the desert sand, every time we dug deep, the sides would cave in. We had two back hoes, a fire unit, an ambulance and MFO MPs [Military Police] deployed, and at one stage an Egyptian house was in danger of falling in as well.

Eventually they were forced to give up and filled in the hole.

Overflying of borders was another problem. Once, it took some fast talking to prevent the Israelis from shooting down a UN helicopter that had strayed.

In between, Sergeant Hartshorn was able to see something of the surrounding countries, including visits to El Alamein in Egypt and other famous battlesites as well as taking a trip down the Nile and visiting the sphinx and pyramids.

Driving conditions were something he commented on in his letters home.

Nothing surprises us in the road any more. Roads with three official lanes will have four or five unofficial lanes, cars jammed together, ignoring red lights (most lights are about to fall over anyway) and one-way signs, trucks driving the wrong way in dual lane carriageways. We even saw a man in a wheel chair sitting in the middle of the right hand lane with traffic whizzing around him.

Sergeant Hartshorn's wife, Corinne, and their two daughters, Vanessa and Natalie, visited the region during his tour of duty. Shortly after he had seen them off on the flight back to Australia, a suicide bomb attack took place on a bus in Dizengoff Square in Tel Aviv in which 22 people were killed and 40 wounded. They had visited the square just a few days earlier.

A woman employee of the MFO had been on the bus but got off 90 seconds before the explosion.

> She recalls seeing a nervous person with a bulky package in his lap. I thank God for our safety, and your prayers, but my heart also goes out to those injured and the families of those killed.

Not all the incident reports received in the Force Duty Centre were serious. At one point, the heaviest rain seen in the region for many years fell steadily.

> The other day, one of the Colombian guards in a tower near our airfield saw two Bedouin trying to steal fencing materials from our perimeter fence. When challenged they fled, with an Egyptian policeman (who patrol outside) hot on their tails. The policeman detained one and took him back to the police shack outside our camp. With all the rain, the Bedouin were probably rebuilding their homes, as they usually have to do after lengthy wet periods.

Supplied by David Hartshorn of Queensland